British Churches

WITH PHOTOGRAPHS FROM
THE FRANCIS FRITH COLLECTION

LOCH ACHRAY, THE TROSSACHS CHURCH 1871 L89001P

British Churches

WITH PHOTOGRAPHS FROM
THE FRANCIS FRITH COLLECTION

Compiled and edited by Eliza Sackett

Bounty
Books

First published in the United Kingdom in 2006 by The Francis Frith Collection for Bounty Books
a division of Octopus Publishing Group,
2-4 Heron Quays, London E14 4JP, England

Hardback edition ISBN 10: 0-7537-1442-6
ISBN 13: 978-0-7537-1442-3

British Library Cataloguing in Publication Data

British Churches
Compiled and edited by Eliza Sackett

The Francis Frith Collection
Frith's Barn, Teffont,
Salisbury, Wiltshire SP3 5QP
Tel: +44 (0) 1722 716 376
Email: info@francisfrith.co.uk
www.francisfrith.com

Designed and assembled by David Davies

Printed in Singapore by Imago

Front Cover: Hitchin, St Mary's Church from Market Place 1908 *60881t*

The colour-tinting in this book is for illustrative purposes only, and is not intended to be historically accurate.

Contents

6   British Churches - An Introduction

7   Styles of Church Architecture and Glossary

8-27   The South West

28-57   The South and London

58–94   The Western Counties and the Midlands

95–112   East Anglia

113–137   The North

138-146   Wales

147-154   Scotland

155   Index

159   Voucher for a free print

British Churches - An Introduction

The church lover must travel with an open mind. We have all passed by churches with unprepossessing exteriors, assuming that there will be little inside worthy of delaying us. And we all know, too, how wrong we can be. We also know that confronting an old prejudice more often than not bears dividends. But the very fact that church lovers do have their own likes and dislikes makes choosing the photographs for a book hazardous!

This book is not intended to be an exhaustive compilation of Britain's finest churches, nor a scholarly account of historical church detail – for that we must as ever turn to Pevsner. These images have been chosen from the world-famous Francis Frith Collection. One of the problems of working with an archive of the size and scope of the Frith Collection is that it is both a treasure house and labyrinth. The sheer number of images can seem overwhelming. We have therefore tried to select photographs that not only depict attractive churches or those with something worth seeing, but that are visually pleasing images in themselves.

Exceptional churches can be found in unexceptional places. It is extraordinary how the smallest of villages often have churches of considerable pomp and grandeur. We must always remember that we are seeing a place a good half a millennium after its church was first conceived and built. Fortunes change, and what looks like a poor, scattered hamlet now could once have been a thriving centre for wool production, for instance. We must remember, too, why some churches are expansive and others modest. It depended very much on local patronage; were there people in the parish prepared to stump up the money to pay for the church? What was the extent of their wealth – and the depth of their piety? Money was always a factor. Many of the photographs in this book show the ornate and impressive family monuments and tombs that perpetuate the memory of the benefactors who paid for the building.

Why do we like a particular church and dislike another? It is rare that one finds a church that is entirely pleasing. The main reason is that most churches have been adapted and altered in a wide variety of styles over the course of many centuries. We are drawn to some of their period features and not others. Sometimes, however, despite being built in a hodge-podge of styles and periods, a church turns out to be an architectural gem – confirming that it is not always homogeneity that impresses.

A very few Saxon churches are included in this book, but in the main the earliest churches that survive in Britain were built by the Normans. The Norman nobles who received vast estates from a grateful William the Conqueror commissioned churches in the style of their homeland. The Norman masons built much larger churches than the Saxons. They built their walls thick and kept the windows small, for larger openings would have weakened the structure. Their arches, following the Roman model, were heavy and semi-circular, and ornately decorated with chevrons and other repetitive motifs. The overall effect was of solid buildings exuding power and authority.

The pointed arch was a revolutionary invention and altered the course of church building throughout Europe. It is fundamental to the Gothic style, and its arrival from the continent in the latter half of the 12th century was to radically change the atmosphere of our churches. Because of its greater strength, the pointed arch could support massive loads and thus allow larger windows and airier arcades. Architects were now able to give their imaginations free rein. Soon they were constructing lofty roofs supported by delicate vaulting resembling branching trees. Below, the broad interiors, often with side aisles, were lit by expansive windows with slim mullions and decorative tracery.

There are three main periods of Gothic building: Early English (1200–1300), Decorated (1300–1350), and Perpendicular (1350–1660). Each has its own individual character, but in general terms, as the centuries progressed interior spaces grew more expansive, windows taller and wider, and roofs higher. Architects employed devices such as supportive buttresses to keep the structure stable.

The period photographs in this book are particularly fascinating because many of them show the churches before modern-day restoration, offering us an insight into how they once looked. It is worth remembering that Victorian zeal changed many of these ancient churches for ever; some used to look positively romantic, swathed in creeper, their towers toppling, their fabric crumbling. During the 18th century some churches had decayed so much that they were even used as farm buildings. Victorian piety, reform and energy reversed all that; a huge amount of 'restoration' was done in the Victorian era, much of which completely effaced the original buildings, making them unrecognisable to their medieval builders. It was as a reaction to this that the Society for the Protection of Ancient Buildings was formed, promoting the respect for ancient fabric that today's restorers have. But before we condemn the Victorians, let us remember that they were almost as prolific church builders as their medieval forebears were, and many of their churches demand our respect and awe.

We hope that this book will inspire you to go out and explore Britain's rich heritage of churches.

'To be insensible to the mute appeal of a building so rich in human pathos is to lose an emotional stimulus, to forgo a spiritual experience, and to neglect an opportunity to enrich our own personalities by developing our powers of imaginative sympathy.'
E A GREENING LAMBORN, 'THE PARISH CHURCH' 1929

Styles of Church Architecture

Norman, Romanesque: 11th and 12th century. Round arches, roll and zigzag mouldings.

Early English: c1190 to c1250. Pointed arches, lancet windows, stiff-leaf carving.

Decorated: c1250 to c1350. Complex window tracery, naturalistic carving, ogee arches.

Perpendicular: c1350 to 1540. Flattened arches, panelled walls and window tracery, large windows.

Glossary

Abacus: flat slab.

Apse: vaulted semicircular or polygonal end of a chancel or chapel.

Arabesque: light and fanciful surface decoration, flowing lines, tendrils, etc, with vases and animals interspersed.

Arcade: range of arches supported on piers or columns, free-standing.

Arch: round headed; semicircular; pointed; segmental; four-centred.

Ashlar: masonry of large blocks with even faces and square edges.

Atrium: inner court or open court in front of a church.

Aumbry: recess or cupboard to hold sacred vessels for Mass and Communion.

Ballflower: decorative carving of small globular flower of three petals enclosing small ball.

Basilica: an aisled church with a clerestory.

Belfry: turret on a roof to hang bells.

Bellcote: framework on a roof to hang bells from.

Block capital: Romanesque capital cut from a cube, lower angles rounded off to a circular shaft below.

Box pew: pew with high wooden enclosure.

Broach spire: usually octagonal, rising from square tower, with triangular face (broach) mediating between the two shapes.

Buttress: mass of brickwork of masonry projecting from or built against a wall for additional strength.

Campanile: isolated bell tower.

Canopy: projection, hood over altar, pulpit, niche, statue, etc.

Capital: head or top of a column.

Cartouche: tablet with ornate frame, usually enclosing inscription.

Castellated: decorated with battlements.

Catslide roof: steep roof almost reaching the ground.

Chamfer: surface made from cutting across the square angle of a stone, or block of wood at an angle of 45 degrees.

Chancel: part of east end of church where altar is placed, applied usually to whole continuation of nave east from the crossing.

Chancel arch: at west end of chancel.

Chantry chapel: attached to, or inside a church for mass for the soul of the founder or other person.

Chevron: Norman moulding forming a zigzag.

Choir: that part of a church where divine service is sung.

Cinquefoil: lobe formed by cusping of a circle or arch - trefoil, quatrefoil, cinquefoil, express the number of leaf shapes.

Clerestory: upper storey of the nave walls of a church, pierced by windows.

Colonnade: range of columns.

Colonette: small column.

Cornice: in classical architecture, the top section of the entablature. Also a decorative feature along top of wall, arch, etc.

Crenellation: battlement.

Cupola: small polygonal or circular domed turret crowning a roof.

Fleche: slender wooden spire on centre of roof.

Fleuron: decorative carved flower or leaf.

Hood mould: projecting moulding above an arch or a lintel to throw off water.

Impost: bracket in a wall.

Keystone: massive stone in an arch or rib vault.

Lancet: narrow window with a pointed arch.

Lucarne: opening to let light in.

Lych gate: wooden gate structure with roof and open sides at entrance to churchyard, providing space for receiving coffins.

Misericord: bracket on underside of hinged choir stall seat - when turned up provides occupant with support during long standing. Also called miserere.

Nailhead: Early English ornamental motif of small pyramids repeated regularly.

Ogee: S-shaped curve, forming arch with pointed top.

Oriel: bay window.

Pediment: low-pitched gable.

Pier: strong solid support.

Pilaster: shallow pier attached to wall.

Piscina: basin for washing Communion or Mass vessels, with drain, set in or against wall to south of altar.

Poppyhead: ornament of leaf and flower decorating tops of bench or stall ends.

Quoins: dressed stones at angles of buildings.

Reredos: structure behind and above altar.

Reticulated tracery: net-like tracery in the top section of a window.

Respond: half pier bonded into wall carrying one end of arch.

Roll moulding: semicircular or more than semicircular section.

Rood: crucifix.

Rood loft: gallery on top of rood screen.

Rood screen: separation between chancel and remainder of church.

Rose window: also wheel window. Circular tracery radiating from centre.

Saltire cross: equal limber cross diagonally placed.

Sedilia: seats for priest on south side of chancel.

Spandrel: triangular surface between side of arch, horizontal drawn from apex and vertical drawn from its springer. Also surface between two arches.

Stiff leaf: Early English type of foliage carving with many-lobed shapes.

Strapwork: 16th-century decoration of interlaced bands, forms similar to fretwork or cut and bent leather.

Tomb chest: stone coffin.

Tourelle: turret corbelled out of wall.

Tracery: intersecting ribwork in upper part of window or decorative work in blank arches, vaults.

Transepts: arms of a church projecting north and south.

Tympanum: space between lintel and arch above doorway.

Wainscot: timber lining to walls.

Waterleaf: leaf shape in later 12th-century capitals, broad, unribbed, tapering curving up towards the angle of the abacus and turned in at top.

Below right: MORWENSTOW, THE CHURCH,
THE FONT 1910 62417

Below: MORWENSTOW, THE CHURCH AND
THE CROSS 1910 62414

Morwenstow

Morwenstow Church. The church of St John the Baptist is remote, a short walk inland from the wild cliffs of Cornwall's windswept north coast. It is famous for Robert Stephen Hawker, who was vicar here for 40 years from 1834. 'Passon' Hawker invented the idea of the harvest festival and celebrated it here, and he buried shipwrecked mariners in his churchyard - the figurehead from the wrecked Scottish brig 'Caledonia' still stands over her captain's grave. Hawker erected the Celtic cross near the churchyard entrance, and the initials CEH carved on its short shaft are those of his first wife Charlotte Eliza. The old cross is believed to have come from north Bodmin Moor, where it may have marked the way for pilgrims.

The superb Norman north arcade with its richly carved capitals and arches (62417, background) is one of the rewarding features of the interior of the church. There are deep chevron designs around the arches, and a carved ram's head can be seen above one of the sturdy round pillars. The more slender south arcade (foreground) is later in date and much plainer. The medieval benches are also particularly fine. The early Norman font, roughly shaped but all the more powerful for that, has an encircling ropework decoration beneath a plain bowl.

Crantock

Above: CRANTOCK,
THE CHURCH 1899 43795

Crantock Church. The foundations of the parish church, dedicated to St Carantoc, are pre-Norman, but the earliest features that we can see today date from Norman times - these are the choir arcades, just visible in the background of 33532 (page 10), and the font (in the foreground). The church became a collegiate church in the 13th century, but the college was closed down at the Dissolution of the Monasteries under Henry VIII. The church was enlarged and altered over the centuries, and restored at the end of the 19th century (by Sedding); photograph 33532 was taken before the restoration, and before the insertion of the rood screen in 1905, which was carved by Mary Rashleigh Pinwell, a vicar's daughter from Devon. The fine stained glass windows (64827 (page 10) tell the story of St Carantoc. In the churchyard is a fine stone coffin (33533, page 10), which may be prehistoric.

Top: CRANTOCK, THE CHURCH, THE INTERIOR 1894   33532

Above: CRANTOCK, STONE COFFIN IN THE CHURCHYARD 1894   33533

Right: CRANTOCK, A CHURCH WINDOW 1912   64827

The village of Crantock is named after the 6th-century St Carantoc. He sailed here from Ireland, bringing a dove with him, which flew inland with a twig in its beak; where the dove dropped the twig, Carantoc decided to build his small oratory.

Polzeath

St Enodoc's Church. The solid little stone tower on a slant, nothing elaborate, dates from the 13th century; it is on the north side of the church, not at the usual west end. The church has Norman origins. Apart from its wonderful location overlooking Daymer Bay and the Camel estuary (Stepper Point is visible at the far side of the estuary in 49953), the church is famous for its being buried by drifting sand dunes; the vicar had to be lowered through the roof to hold services. At last St Enodoc's was dug out and restored in 1864. Note the Cornish cross memorials and tomb chests in the churchyard.

This area of Cornwall was much loved by the Poet Laureate Sir John Betjeman. This was his holiday home as a boy and as an adult, and he was buried in the churchyard in 1984. His mother was buried here too, and there is a memorial to his father inside the church.

Above: POLZEATH, ST ENODOC'S CHURCH 1903 49953

Below: POLZEATH, ST ENODOC'S CHURCH C1960 P70139

Today, St Enodoc's stands in the middle of a golf course, and visitors have to be wary of flying golf balls. This is how John Betjeman described the way to the church:

'Paths, unfamiliar to golfers' brogues,
Cross the eleventh fairway broadside on
And leave the fourteenth tee for thirteenth green,
Ignoring Royal and Ancient, bound for God.'

LISKEARD, OLD TOMBSTONE C1960 L53075

Liskeard

Lostwithiel

St Bartholomew's Church. There has probably been a church here from ancient times; the present building dates from the end of the 12th century. The tower and spire, 'the pre-eminent glory of the West of England', were begun in the 13th century; at the lowest stage of the tower are stout buttresses, then narrow lancets, and then a striking octagonal lantern, which is topped by eight traceried gables which surround the spire. The church has a vast east window, now filled with 19th-century glass.

The font of St Bartholomew's (32584) is from the 14th century, octagonal, and finely carved in high relief with alarming human heads, a huntsman, a wolf and other creatures. The church was desecrated by troops in the Civil War, and the font was used to christen a horse – he was given the name Charles.

Above left: LOSTWITHIEL, ST BARTHOLOMEW'S CHURCH 1893 32581

Left: LOSTWITHIEL, ST BARTHOLOMEW'S CHURCH, THE FONT 1893 32584

Dartmouth

St Saviour's Church. St Saviour's was founded by Edward I in 1286, and it was enlarged and rebuilt in the 15th and 17th centuries. The rebuilding in the 15th century was undertaken by John Hawley, a merchant, an adventurer, and the model for the English sailor in Chaucer's 'Canterbury Tales'. As late as 1567 ships were still being tied up to the churchyard wall, for the churchyard overlooked the harbour. The imposing door in the south porch is decorated with 13th-century ironwork, including images of two leopards with the tree of life. The hinges holding the whole structure together are said to date from 1631. The old keyhole is concealed in a leaf.

DARTMOUTH, ST SAVIOUR'S CHURCH, THE DOOR 1896 38906

Widecombe -in-the-Moor

The following account of a terrible storm at Widecombe in 1683 is given in 'Worthies of Devon' by John Prince (1643-1723):

'In the afternoon in service time, there happened a very great darkness, which still increased to that degree, that they could not see to read, soon after a terrible and fearful thunder was heard, like the noise of so many great guns, accompanied with dreadful lightning, to the great amazement of the people; the darkness still increasing, that they could not see each other, when there presently came such an extraordinary flame of lightning, as filled the Church with flame, smoke and a loathsome smell, like brimstone; a ball of fire came in likewise at the window, and passed through the Church, which so affrighted the congregation that most of them fell down in their seats, some upon their knees, others upon their faces, and some one upon another, crying out of burning and scalding, and all giving themselves up for dead. There were in all four persons killed and sixty-two hurt, divers of them having their linen burnt, tho' the outward garments were not so much as singed. ... The Church itself was much torn and defaced with the thunder and lightning, a beam whereof breaking in the midst, fell down between the minister and clerk, and hurt neither. The steeple was much rent, and it was observed where the Church was most torn there was the least hurt was done among the people. There was none hurt with the timber or stone, but one man who, it was judged, was killed by a fall of stone.'

The Church of St Pancras. The noble Perpendicular granite tower of Widecombe's church stands out against the austere hills of Dartmoor rising behind it. For centuries this tower has been a landmark and beacon for travellers on the moor, and today the splendid church is not eclipsed by the commercialisation of this popular tourist village – for this is where old Uncle Tom Cobley and all, riding on Tom Pearce's grey mare, come on their ghostly trip to Widecombe Fair.

Inside the wide, spacious church is the base of a rood screen painted with 32 saints, and a plain granite arcade paces down towards the altar. On the ceiling are painted bosses, including one showing three rabbits with only three ears between them. This has been said to be an emblem of the tin miners. This tradition originated in the 19th century, when an engraving dating from c1660 was found; entitled 'The Hunt of Venus', it showed the three rabbits encircled by hounds and the chemical signs of various metals, including tin. However, the rabbits are in fact a very ancient symbol – they have been found on various artefacts from China and India dating from the 6th century, and in many other European countries too. Perhaps they symbolise the Trinity here.

Above left: WIDECOMBE-IN-THE-MOOR, THE CHURCH OF ST PANCRAS AND THE VILLAGE 1927 79792

Swimbridge

St James's Church. Swimbridge is a picturesque village lying in a cup of rounded, rolling hills near Barnstaple. The long, low body of the church, built in the Perpendicular style, is typical of the West Country, but the arresting 90ft spire is not – it is one of only three medieval spires in North Devon. Amongst the most interesting features of this church are its fittings, many of them visible in 45725. What is left of the ceiling is panelled and painted, and studded with bosses. The stone pulpit dates from c1490 – it still bears traces of medieval paint. The splendid richly ornamented rood screen stretches across nave and aisles, carved with foliage, its arches fan-vaulted. The most remarkable object of all is the font cover (right foreground of 45725), a kind of cupboard (doors can close round the font) crowned with Gothic openwork with a canopy over it, a highly unusual arrangement.

Above: SWIMBRIDGE,
ST JAMES'S CHURCH 1894 33428

Opposite page: SWIMBRIDGE,
ST JAMES'S CHURCH, THE INTERIOR
1900 45725

The pulpit here at St James's was occupied for forty-six years from 1833 by Jack Russell, the famous hunting parson. His sermons were by Victorian standards blessedly brief, as his horse was usually saddled and waiting in the churchyard for him to go hunting. The story goes that the Bishop of Exeter asked Mr Russell to sell his pack of hounds, since hunting parsons were bringing ridicule to the church. The vicar agreed – and transferred his pack to his wife's name and carried on hunting. His biggest claim to fame, however, is the breeding of the terrier named after him. The local pub is also the Jack Russell, and Jack Russell terrier societies meet here.

Mortehoe

It is said that one tomb inside Mortehoe church holds the bones of William de Tracey, one of the four murderers of Thomas Becket, though some historians have cast doubt upon the tale. What is certain is that the de Traceys held land in the area at around this period.

Above: MORTEHOE, THE CHURCH 1935 87130P

Left: MORTEHOE, THE CHURCH, THE INTERIOR 1935 87131

Mortehoe Church. The 13th-century Church of St Mary Magdalene, founded by a priest named William de Tracey, stands opposite the local pub, named the Ship Aground in memory of the many ships that met their end on nearby Morte Point. The close proximity of church and inn is common in rural parishes, giving worshippers the chance of refreshment before the long walk back home.

The enormous mosaic above the chancel arch was created in 1905 in memory of the churchwarden's wife. The churchwarden in question must have been a wealthy man, for the magnificent depiction of archangels was designed by Selwyn Image and made by the same craftsmen responsible for the mosaics in St Paul's Cathedral. Selwyn Image (1849-1930) attended lectures given by John Ruskin. Together with the architect Mackmurdo, he was a founder member of the Century Guild, a pioneering and highly influential Arts and Crafts organisation. From 1910 to 1916 he was Professor of Fine Arts at Oxford. This mosaic at Mortehoe is therefore a highly important example of Arts and Crafts design.

Taunton

St Mary Magdalene's Church. The wealth that was created in Taunton in the Middle Ages by both agriculture and the cloth industry was often spent on the construction of fine buildings, especially churches and their soaring towers. A Perpendicular style of church towers developed in Somerset, which is distinctive enough for them to be known as 'Somerset Towers'. The 163ft-high tower of St Mary Magdalene's Church, built of Old Red Quantock sandstone and Ham Hill stone, dominates the skyline of Taunton. It is one of the most beautiful of many exquisite church towers in Somerset, despite being a reconstruction. The rebuild of the tower was completed in 1862, to the lines of the original 15th-century design. During the rebuild of the tower of St Mary Magdalene's Church, a donkey powered the pulley which took up the stone to the workmen. When the work was completed in 1862, the donkey was taken up to the top of the tower to admire the view!

The south chancel window in the church at Hatch Beauchamp, just off the A358 between Taunton and Ilminster, is dedicated to John Chard VC, who died in the village. Chard was the commanding officer at the battle of Rorke's Drift in the Zulu Wars - he was immortalised in the popular film 'Zulu', in which he was played by the actor Stanley Baker.

Above: TAUNTON, ST MARY MAGDALENE'S CHURCH 1888 20859

Bishop's Hull

Above: BISHOP'S HULL, THE CHURCH 1906 55810

The Church of St Peter and St Paul at Bishop's Hull is unusual – it has one of Somerset's octagonal towers. Buried in the churchyard is William Crotch, a self-taught musical prodigy who became the first principal of the Royal Academy of Music in 1822.

Glastonbury

During Henry VIII's Dissolution of the Monasteries, the Tor was the site where the last Abbot of Glastonbury, Richard Whiting, and two fellow monks were hanged, drawn and quartered for 'treason' - they resisted Henry's changes.

In Christ Church, Bristol, on Thomas Turner, twice
Master of the Company of Bakers:

Like to a Baker's oven is the grave,
Wherein the bodies of the faithful have
A setting in, and where they do remain
In hopes to rise, and to be drawn again:
Blessed are they who in the Lord are dead;
Though set like dough, they shall be drawn like bread.

Left: GLASTONBURY, ST MICHAEL'S TOWER 1896 38383

St Michael's Tower. Glastonbury Tor rises like a cone from the Levels. As a landmark the Tor is enhanced considerably by the tower on its top. In legend, Glastonbury Tor has been said to be a hollow hill, one of the entrances to the Underworld, and the home of the Lord of the Underworld, Gwyn ap Nudd. The tor has also been linked with King Arthur's Isle of Avalon, reminding us that in the past, when the area was even more prone to flooding than it is today, the Tor must have looked like an island in the Levels. Even today, on a winter's morning when the Tor looms above a landscape wreathed in mist, it is hard not to feel affected by a sense of timeless mystery.

Archaeologists have found evidence of occupation on the Tor in prehistory and during the Roman period. There was also occupation in the centuries after the Romans left; was this was a defended civil settlement, perhaps the stronghold of a local chieftain? It seems more likely that it was a monastic site pre-dating Glastonbury's abbey, perhaps a hermitage or a retreat. After the abbey was founded in the early 8th century, the Tor continued to be used by hermits - the church of St Michael was built in the 13th century as a pilgrims' chapel. The dedication of the church on the Tor to St Michael, the archangel who defeated the dragon (symbolic of the Devil), shows that Christians saw the Tor as a site of great pagan significance which needed the protection of their most powerful saint.

Bristol

Left: BRISTOL, THE CHURCH OF
ST MARY REDCLIFFE 1887 20153

In the churchyard of St Mary
Redcliffe is a memorial to the
church cat, who used to sit on
the organist's lap and listen to
the music.

The Church of St Mary Redcliffe. The church of St Mary Redcliffe in Bristol is as large as a cathedral, and is one of only two parish churches in England to have stone vaulting. St Mary's was built on a large scale thanks to the generosity of Bristol merchants. The glorious spire is 292ft high, the astonishing north porch is almost oriental in the splendour of its stone carving, and the Perpendicular piers soar upwards to the complex stone vaulting, which is adorned with 1,200 bosses. The name Redcliffe derives from the red sandstone outcrop upon which St Mary's stands; the church itself is built of oolitic limestone. The church was visited by Elizabeth I in 1574, who described it as the 'fairest and goodliest' church in England, although she was less impressed with the Bristol women -'Good Lord, master Mayor, how plain the women of Bristol be!'

The church houses some interesting artefacts, including what is purported to be a rib from the Dun Cow said to have been slain by Guy of Warwick; it is in fact a whalebone, thought to have been presented by the explorer John Cabot, who in 1497 set sail from Bristol and discovered mainland north America. In front of the high altar of St Mary Redcliffe is a brass to John Brooke and his wife Johanna. She was the daughter of Richard Amerycke, collector for customs and patron of John Cabot. So just who was America named after?

Toller Porcorum

Above: TOLLER PORCORUM, THE CHURCH OF ST ANDREW AND ST PETER 1906 54557

Left: TOLLER PORCORUM, THE CHURCH OF ST ANDREW AND ST PETER, THE FONT 1906 54558

The Church of St Andrew and St Peter. This remote settlement (whose name means stream of the pigs - wild boar were kept in the oak woods which once grew right up to the edge of the village) lies under the downs that pitch and roll all the way from Beaminster to Dorchester. The church perches on a hillock in the midst of the village. The short tower, which dates from 1300, has gargoyles under its battlements. From the outside, the south aisle, built in 1833, looks as if it was tacked on to the 13th- and 14th-century fabric with little thought for architectural composition; its arcade was restored in 1891. However, once you have entered the church (by the west door under the tower and a ringing gallery), the architect's conception is immediately apparent: the south aisle brings the church a remarkable feeling of space, making the floor area almost square, and allowing light to flood in through its three large windows, from which you can see glimpses of the downs beyond. The atmosphere is friendly and close to domestic, marred only by some obtrusively dark mortaring. The base of the font is a large Norman capital in white stone, with volutes and a ram's head on one corner. Some say the pedestal is older and was once part of a Roman altar.

St Mary's Church. This view shows Frampton and its church in more peaceful times; nowadays traffic thunders around the awkward corner encircling the south aisle en route to Dorchester. The thick creeper smothering the tower in the photograph made it impossible for the Edwardian villagers to see one of the great wonders of this originally 15th-century building. When the creeper was removed, where one would have expected to see Perpendicular-style buttresses, extraordinary Tuscan columns were uncovered: in 1695, Robert Browne of Frampton Court was determined to build an ecclesiastical building that was modish and in the fashionable classical style. The matching aisles have attractive openwork parapets, and their width makes the building seem much bigger than it looks from the outside. The north aisle of 1820 is enriched with magnificent monuments and wall tombs, mainly of the 18th century. The chancel, with its elaborate timber roof, was rebuilt by Ferrey in 1862, and at its east end is a fancy reredos with gilt and coloured mosaic.

Frampton

Above: FRAMPTON, ST MARY'S CHURCH 1906 54585

Above: STINSFORD, ST MICHAEL'S CHURCH 1930 83397

Left: STINSFORD, ST MICHAEL'S CHURCH, THOMAS HARDY'S GRAVE 1930 83398

Stinsford

St Michael's Church. Though only a modest hamlet, tucked away at the edge of the great park of Kingston Maurward House, Stinsford is at the very heart of Hardy's Wessex. Stinsford is the Mellstock of his 'Under the Greenwood Tree', but the gallery where Mellstock village choir and band pumped out their invigorating rustic music was removed around 1900. The church, described by Hardy as being of 'various styles from Transition-Norman to late Perpendicular', has a plain, unembellished exterior and unbuttressed tower, and is of mainly 13th- and 15th-century origins. Outside is an imposing Saxon relief depicting St Michael with outspread wings. Inside, the chancel arch is imposing, its mouldings deeply carved, and there is a splendid two-bay south aisle with grotesque 'gurgoyles' - Hardy wrote about them in 'Far From the Madding Crowd'. Hardy was born just two miles away at Higher Bockhampton, and there is a window to his memory in the church. Hardy's ashes are buried in Poets' Corner, Westminster Abbey, but his heart is buried in the long, low tomb in Stinsford's churchyard.

Worth Matravers

No visitor should leave Worth Matravers without visiting square, buttressed St Aldhelm's chapel, lonely and dark on its wave-lashed headland, its austere Norman arches rising into the gloom from a single central column.

St Nicholas's Church. Worth Matravers lies in Purbeck, where for centuries the Purbeck limestone was quarried from the cliffs and transported all over Britain. Naturally, the village houses are built of Purbeck stone, and so is the church. The churchyard's most celebrated grave is that of farmer Benjamin Jesty, who retired to Dunshay Manor from Yetminster. There he had pioneered vaccination by introducing cowpox by inoculation to protect his family from smallpox.

This is one of the Isle of Purbeck's most ancient churches; stone-roofed, its proportions long and low, it has withstood the gales from the sea for hundreds of years. It was built by the Normans, and around the outside walls a corbel-table with carved heads runs beneath the eaves. The south doorway, similar in style to the one at Studland, another sea-girt Norman church, has a tympanum depicting the Coronation of the Virgin. Inside, the chancel arch is richly carved with typically Norman zigzag decoration, while the chancel itself was altered in the 13th century, and a fine east window was inserted in the 14th century.

Left: WORTH MATRAVERS, ST NICHOLAS'S CHURCH
1899 43790

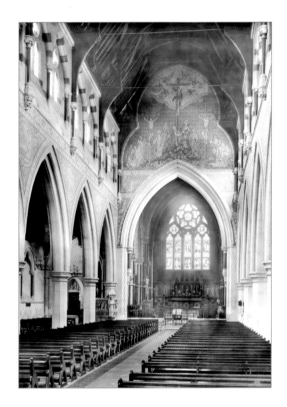

Above: BOURNEMOUTH, ST PETER'S CHURCH, THE
INTERIOR 1890   25509

Right: BOURNEMOUTH, ST PETER'S CHURCH AND
THE CEMETERY 1890   25512

The wall paintings in St Peter's are frescoes, and
were innovative in that no lime was used, the
colours being mixed with an adhesive preparation
of gelatine to ensure their permanence.

St Peter's Church. This prime example of lavish Victorian Gothic was built by G E Street over a period of 25 years, and was finally finished in 1880. Although hemmed in now by department stores and busy town centre traffic, the church fights back spiritedly, its spire soaring over the town. The first impression one gets is the sheer size of the building: the nave is long, and the timber roof rises high above the clerestory. The other most striking thing is the sheer amount of rich decoration, especially the wall paintings (by Clayton and Bell, 1873) over the chancel arch and in the spandrels of the arcades. The vaulted chancel ceiling is also painted in a dark rich green with golden angels swinging incense to designs by G F Bodley. Magnificent wrought iron and brass screens separate the chancel from the nave and transepts. The south transept, now the Keble chapel, is also lavishly painted - John Keble, the great Victorian priest and poet, stayed in Bournemouth in 1865-66 and walked each day through the pleasure gardens to worship here. At the west end, the open-work in the spandrels of the tower arch with their curious curving forms is reminiscent of the great strainer arches in Wells Cathedral.

The cemetery (25512) has a romantic hillside setting with many fine trees; here stands the vault of the Shelley family, containing the heart of the poet Percy Bysshe Shelley; here also are buried his wife Mary Shelley, author of 'Frankenstein', and her parents, the authors William Godwin and Mary Wollstonecraft.

Kinson

St Andrew's Church. Before Bournemouth was developed, the heathland and coastline of the area was much frequented by smugglers. The tower of St Andrew's Church at Kinson was used for storing contraband, and ledges on the tower have been damaged by the hauling up of kegs with ropes. In the churchyard is the grave of Robert Trotman, a smuggler shot dead by the customs officers in 1765. The epitaph on his tomb reads:

To the Memory of ROBERT TROTMAN
Late of Rond [ie Rowde] in the County
Of Wilts who was barbarously
Murder'd on the Shore near
Poole the 24 March 1765

A little Tea one leaf I did not steal
For Guiltless Blood shed I to GOD appeal
Put Tea in one scale human Blood in tother
And think what tis to slay thy harmless Brother

Left: KINSON, ST ANDREW'S CHURCH 1955 K115010

Here sleeps in peace a Hampshire grenadier,
Who caught his death by drinking cold, small beer.
Soldiers! Take heed from his untimely fall,
And when you're hot, drink strong, or none at all!

To which these words were later added:
An honest soldier never is forgot,
Whether he die by musket or by pot.

WINCHESTER CATHEDRAL,
THOMAS THETCHER'S HEADSTONE 1906   55866

Kings Worthy

KINGS WORTHY, ST MARY'S CHURCH 1912 64468P

Above: KINGS WORTHY, ST MARY'S CHURCH 1912 64469

St Mary's Church. Inside this fine church is an ancient font which dates back over 500 years, and a window in the side chapel contains a small round panel of medieval glass depicting two mitred bishops with croziers drawn in gold. A commemorative tablet recalls the names of four brothers who were killed in the Great War. In the main entrance is a colourful tapestry depicting the village, made by more than 30 people.

In the churchyard is an inscription on one of the headstones in memory of James Parker, who was brutally murdered in 1886. The headstone provides an intriguing clue to the way he died, and is a quotation from the Bible: 'The enemy hath smitten my life down to the ground'. Parker was a young seaman; having just arrived in Southampton, he set off on foot for London with another member of the ship's crew. They called at a tavern on the way, and the next morning Parker's battered body was found in a field. His companion took a train to the capital, where he was arrested and charged with murder. The man later confessed to the crime, revealing at the same time where the murder weapons were hidden. The money for the headstone was donated by local residents.

Bentley

Left: BENTLEY, THE CHURCH
1929 82440

Below: BENTLEY, THE CHURCH AND
YEW TREES 1929 82439

Yew Trees

Britain has more ancient yews than most other countries, many of them in churchyards. This is because from ancient times, all over the world, the yew has been associated with death, rebirth and immortality; in many cultures it is the tree of life (a concept which can be traced back to Neolithic times), and associated with the mother goddess, and some traditions link the yew with the tree of knowledge. Celtic, Nordic and Anglo-Saxon myths share this belief in the yew as the tree of death and rebirth, and hence yew trees would have been planted in sacred places, particularly burial places, as the protector of the soul during its transition from death to eternal life. When Christianity came to Britain, it took over the sacred places of the old religion, and indeed the symbolism of the yew fitted very well with the Christian message of resurrection; thus a new Christian church would be built beside the sacred yew. How fitting it is that today yew trees are the source of life-giving anti-cancer drugs.

Bentley Church. The name 'Bentley' means 'woodland clearing where bent-grass grows'. The low tower of St Mary's Church can just be seen against a curtain of trees in photograph 82440. The base is over 500 years old, while the top is more recent. The oldest parts of the church are Norman, and are built of malm stone probably quarried locally. The font is Norman too; it was found nearby in a farmyard about a hundred years ago. The south chapel and south arcade were added in the 13th century; the pillars are incised with consecration crosses, probably put there when the church was re-consecrated after the neglect caused by the Black Death in 1348-49. Some of the pillars are scratched with pilgrim crosses as well, for Bentley lies on a pilgrim route to Canterbury.

The beautiful avenue of yew trees (82439) leads up to the church. The trees are considered to be at least 500 years old, and considering the age of the church, they may well be older – see the box about yew trees (above).

Eversley

Above: EVERSLEY, ST MARY'S CHURCH AND THE LYCHGATE 1901 46838

Left: EVERSLEY, ST MARY'S CHURCH 1901 46841

Eversley Church. There is a tangible air of mystery about Eversley church. Inside, among other fascinating features, is a sarsen stone hidden beneath a trap door. The stone, discovered in 1940, could be part of the foundations of a heathen place of worship. The Victorian author and Christian socialist Charles Kingsley (1819-75), who wrote 'The Water Babies' and 'Westward Ho!', was rector here for many years. A few yards from the door of Eversley church lies the grave of Charles Kingsley. His wife Fanny lies with him, and above the grave is a striking white marble cross with the words 'God is love' inscribed on it. The foliage is not so thick today, and neat paths and manicured lawns surround the church.

Fanny Kingsley wrote of early difficulties at Eversley thus:

'[Charles Kingsley] and his wife now settled in the Rectory at Eversley; and life flowed on peacefully, notwithstanding the anxieties of a sorely neglected parish, and the expenses of an old house which had not been repaired for more than a hundred years. Owing to the circumstances under which the living fell vacant, the incoming tenant got no dilapidation-money, and had arrears of poor rates and the pay of his predecessor's curate to meet. The house was damp and unwholesome, surrounded with ponds, which overflowed with every heavy rain, and flooded not only the garden and stables, but all the rooms on the ground floor, keeping up master and servants sometimes all night baling out the water in buckets for hours together; and drainage works had to be done before it was habitable.'

FROM 'CHARLES KINGSLEY: HIS LETTERS AND MEMORIES. EDITED BY HIS WIFE' 1879

Winchfield

Above: WINCHFIELD, THE CHURCH OF ST MARY THE VIRGIN 1904 51238

Right: WINCHFIELD, THE CHURCH INTERIOR 1908 60084

Winchfield Church. This delightful little Norman church is known for its red roof and red-capped tower. Its superb Norman doorway has richly carved sides and arches and distinctive fern leaves round its capitals. The churchyard is pleasantly sheltered by trees. The elaborately decorated south door leads into the church, illuminated by narrow windows decorated round the edges with zigzag carving. The chancel arch too is richly ornamented with roll mouldings and zigzag carvings (60084); the chancel itself is so small that there is only room for two small benches. To the right is the striking 17th-century pulpit, richly carved with cherubs and vases of flowers. The ancient oak pew in front of the pulpit possibly dates back over 700 years. The font is Norman, with pillars of Purbeck marble at its base. Behind it is a plain Norman tower arch.

Bonchurch

A local legend of St Boniface tells that he once had doubts about his faith. Here at Bonchurch he went down to the sea and prayed to God for a sign. Nearby a boy was digging a hole in the sand and trying to fill it with seawater – but the water ran away through the sand, and the boy was crying in frustration. Boniface asked why he was so upset, and the boy replied, 'I'm trying to empty the sea into the hole, but I can't!' Boniface immediately understood the cause of his doubts: he had been trying to fit the infinite inside his finite mind.

The Church of St Boniface. Bonchurch is a strikingly picturesque village between the sea and a steep down smothered in green trees. From the early 19th century Bonchurch was highly fashionable with well-to-do visitors, and it expanded quickly, with villas marching relentlessly over the down.

The ancient church of St Boniface, just 48ft long and with space for only 80 worshippers, was too small for the growing community, but it was mercifully spared from the restorers: in the late 1840s a new church was built. Thus the atmosphere of the old church remained romantic and sublime, bosky and damp, with a stream purling by, and water cascading down to the sea below. After the old church became deserted, it fell into a long sleep. Ivy colonised the porch and roofs, and creeper wound its way over the old fabric, as we can see in the photograph.

The poet Swinburne was born in 1837 at East Dene, a long, low house set close by the church. He spent many hours wandering the paths of the old overgrown churchyard, and the wooded slopes of the down. His evocative poem 'A Forsaken Garden' summons up the deeply romantic atmosphere here:

> *'In a coign of the cliff between lowland and highland,*
> *At the sea-down's edge between windward and lee, …*
> *If a step should sound or a word be spoken,*
> *Would a ghost not rise at the strange guest's hand? …*
> *Through branches and briars if a man make way,*
> *He shall find no life but the restless sea-wind's*
> *Night and day.'*

Swinburne died in 1909 and was buried here in the old overgrown churchyard of St Boniface.

Left: BONCHURCH, THE CHURCH OF ST BONIFACE 1890 26153

Shere

Above: SHERE, THE CHURCH 1904 51793

Shere Church. Shere is a picturesque village on the Tillingbourne, a favourite destination for cyclists in the 19th century and a magnet for tourists ever since. Indeed, the beautiful broach spire of St James's Church may well have attracted earlier travellers, pilgrims travelling to Canterbury along the downs above the village. St James's mainly dates from the 12th century, with the south aisle and the top of the tower from the 13th century.

The church in Shere is famous for its 14th-century anchorite, or hermit, Christine: she was the local carpenter's daughter, and she was twice walled up in her cell against the wall of the church. After three years of holy imprisonment, she left her cell in 1332 – an unprecedented thing to do, for an anchorite was supposed to stay imprisoned until death. Christine later wanted to return to her cell, and the bishop permitted her to be 'thrust back into the said re-enclosure … that she may learn how nefarious was her committed sin'. The remains of her cell are outside the north wall of the chancel.

Wotton

Above: WOTTON, THE CHURCH OF ST JOHN THE EVANGELIST 1919 68828

Wotton Church. An interesting local custom takes place every February when the Forty-Shilling Day contest is held in Wotton, near Dorking. This was set up by William Glanville in 1711, who left 40 shillings each for five poor boys of the parish under the age of sixteen who were willing and able to recite the Lord's Prayer, the Apostles' Creed and the Ten Commandments 'in a plain and audible voice' whilst standing with their right hands placed upon Glanville's tomb in St John's churchyard.

John Evelyn (1620-1706), the noted diarist, and a founder member of the Royal Society, was born at Wotton, and he and his wife are buried in the Evelyn Chapel of St John's Church alongside many other members of the Evelyn family.

As we can see from the photograph, St John's is beautifully situated among large trees. Its charming squat tower is 11th-century, and the rest of the church is 13th-century.

Newdigate

St Peter's Church. St Peter's Church at Newdigate, with its 14th-century tower made entirely out of wood and supported inside by a framework of huge oak timbers, also has a 13th-century chancel and a south aisle added 100 years later, with a peephole from one to the other. Below the octagonal shingled spire is a belfry containing six bells whose sound, ringing out across the countryside, has made Newdigate renowned among campanologists.

Above: NEWDIGATE, THE CHURCH 1906   53536P

Right: FARNHAM, ST ANDREW'S CHURCH AND LOWER CHURCH LANE 1904   51607

Opposite: FARNHAM, ST ANDREW'S CHURCH, WILLIAM COBBETT'S GRAVE 2004   F11717K

Farnham

St Andrew's Church owns a Vinegar Bible, presented in 1739 by Arthur Onslow, Speaker of the House of Commons. Vinegar Bibles get their name from a misprint in St Luke's Gospel: the parable of the vineyard becomes 'the parable of the vinegar'.

St Andrew's Church. The remarkable, self-taught William Cobbett, who was born in Farnham in 1763 and was buried there in 1835, embarked on an epic series of horseback journeys across southern England between 1821 and 1826; he published his account of these in his 'Rural Rides', which provide a fascinating record of country life and landscape at this period. A radical politician, a prolific writer and a great humanist, Cobbett railed against the many social injustices he saw around him: corrupt landlords and absentee estate owners, the plight of the agricultural workforce, the lack of democratic parliamentary representation, and the pernicious influence of the spreading metropolis of London, which he detested and called 'the Great Wen'.

St Andrew's Church was built in the 11th century on the site of a Saxon church, and it was enlarged between the 13th and the 15th centuries. There is some fine stained glass, a 14th-century oak screen, and a plaque in memory of Augustus Toplady, who wrote the hymn 'Rock of Ages' – he was born in Farnham in 1740.

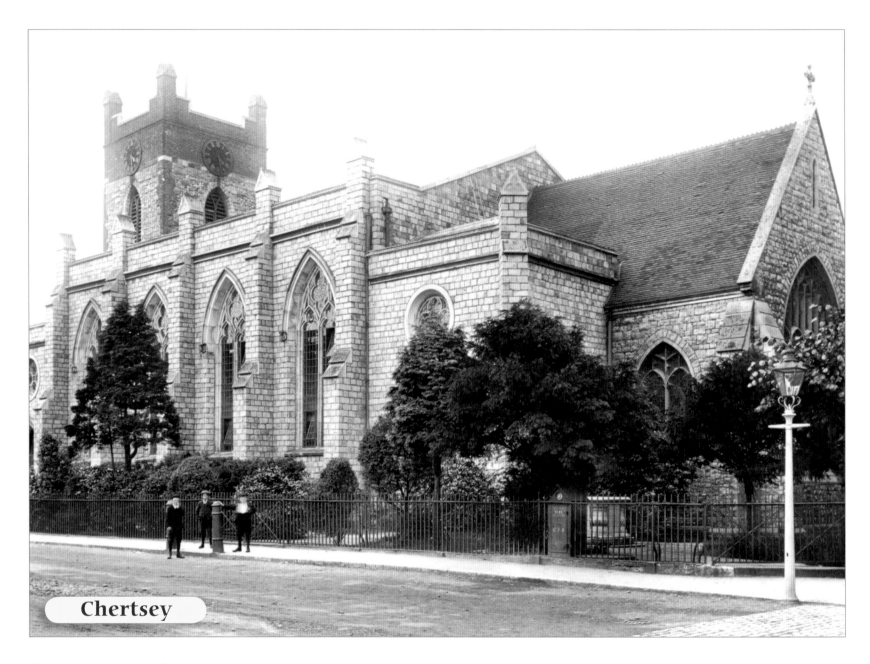

Chertsey

Above: CHERTSEY, ST PETER'S CHURCH 1904 51721P

St Peter's Church. St Peter's Church at Chertsey is famous for the story of Blanche Heriot, a heroine from the time of the Wars of the Roses. Her lover, a nephew of the Earl of Warwick, was captured by the Yorkists and was condemned to be executed when the curfew bell tolled. Although a messenger was sent to the king asking for him to be reprieved, no reply had been received by the time the bell was due to ring. In an attempt to save her lover, Blanche climbed the church tower and hung on to the clapper of the bell so that it could not be rung. Her resourcefulness paid off, as the reprieve arrived an hour after the curfew should have been rung. As a schoolgirl, the American poet Rose Hartwick Thorpe was inspired by this story and wrote a popular ballad about it called 'Curfew Must Not Ring Tonight'.

All but the tower and chancel of St Peter's was rebuilt in the Gothic style in 1806-08. The window-frames and mullions are made of artificial stone, and the columns are iron pillars encased in wood.

Above: SOUTH HARTING, THE CHURCH AND THE VILLAGE 1906 54413

Anthony Trollope, the Victorian novelist, lived in the village of South Harting for many years, and is buried here.

South Harting

The Church of St Mary and St Gabriel. South Harting is a large village at the western end of the Sussex Downs. The church of St Mary and St Gabriel has a broach spire on a central tower, the spire covered with copper. The church mainly dates from the 13th century, with rather austere nave arcades, but there are elaborate Elizabethan timber roofs, inserted after a fire. A substantial oak spiral staircase winds from the north transept to the belfry. A spectacular painted tomb commemorating the Cowper family stands in the south transept: John Cowper and his wife lie in formal Elizabethan dress, while the father kneels above. During the Civil War the Caryll Chapel was desecrated by the Royalists in 1643 and then by the Parliamentarians, and left in ruins. In the churchyard is a war memorial carved by the renowned sculptor Eric Gill.

Above: TILLINGTON, ALL HALLOWS' CHURCH 1912 64899

All Hallows' Church. The coronet design on the tower of All Hallows' Church in Tillington, near Midhurst, is the only one of its kind in Sussex, and is rarely found in this country. The early 19th-century design is distinguished by flying buttresses at the four corners, meeting in a finial and forming a Scots crown. The architect is not known.

Bosham Church. Bosham is not directly on the sea, but at the end of an arm from Chichester harbour. In this view (opposite) we look past the fishermen, nowadays replaced by leisure yachtsmen, to the Anglo-Saxon church, beyond the greensward known as Quay Meadow. Like so many Sussex churches, Holy Trinity has a shingled spire, so characteristic of the county. The wooden shingles are thin 'slates' of oak, which are cleft, not sawn. They should last for about a hundred years. At the east end of the church is a fine group of five lancet windows dating from the 13th century. The church is believed to be the burial place of King Canute's second daughter, who died in infancy.

This present-day fishing village and yachting centre was once a place of much greater importance. The Romans, the Saxons and the Vikings (who stole the church bells) used the area for invasion, and King Canute had a palace here. Bosham is traditionally the place where the king tried to hold back the tide, in an effort to prove to his fawning courtiers that he was not all-powerful as they suggested.

Bosham

Above: BOSHAM, HOLY TRINITY CHURCH AND THE GREEN 1903   50919P

Bosham features on the Bayeux Tapestry, for in 1064 King Edward the Confessor's brother-in-law Harold Godwinson (later King Harold) sailed from Bosham to Normandy, and set in train the events that led to the Battle of Hastings and his own death. Harold is depicted on the tapestry praying in Bosham church for a safe passage before setting out on his journey. It is not clear whether Harold's visit was accident or design - some accounts say that Edward had sent Harold to see William, but others say that Harold only ended up in Normandy after being shipwrecked. As we can see on the Bayeux Tapestry, Harold agreed (or was forced) to swear on holy relics that after King Edward's death he would uphold William's claim to the English throne. When Harold broke this vow, William made this one of his justifications for invading England. Because a sacred vow appeared to have been broken, William was also able to call upon the support of the Pope.

AN ARTIST'S IMPRESSION OF A NORMAN SHIP, FROM THE BAYEUX TAPESTRY   F6019

Yapton

Above: YAPTON, THE CHURCH 1898 42567

The Church of St Mary. The village of Yapton lies between Bognor Regis and Littlehampton, and boasts this fascinating and intriguing church, a jumble of architectural styles and unusual angles. The shingled tower leans one way and the porch leans another (the porch, the west window above it, and the crown post roof of the nave are the newest parts of the church, dating from the 15th century). The Church of St Mary was probably begun at the beginning of the 13th century, when the tower and the nave arcades were built (but possibly older masonry at the base of the tower suggests that it was built on the site of an older building). The nave and aisles are covered by a steep catslide roof which ends up only three feet off the ground. The leaning tower is supported by buttresses of brick and stone built in the 17th century, when the charming dormer windows were inserted.

St Margaret's Church. This tombstone and its charming verses commemorate Michael Turner (1796-1885), clerk and sexton of Warnham for 50 years, a real character and a village institution. A contemporary account tells us that he was something of a dandy, always dressed 'in true Sussex style – smock frock, breeches, and gaiters; and on Sundays he wore a clean white smock, high hat, and top boots'. As well as clerk and sexton, he was leader of the church choir; he sat facing the congregation in the rood loft, leading the singing with his violin, singing himself, and nodding his head to keep time. He would also play and sing at village festivals and at balls at the big houses – 'he would perform a first-rate jig playing his fiddle the while, or sing a capital comic song.' He died with his fiddle in his arms, 'his constant companion to the last'.

Lullington

Lullington Church. This tiny flint and stone church stands on the South Downs above Alfriston and the River Cuckmere. The church dates from the 12th century and is one of the smallest churches in England. It measures only about 16ft square, and is capable of housing only some 20 worshippers – any more that come have to sit in the churchyard. As there is no electricity, services are only held in the summer. It is in fact the surviving chancel of a larger building (mainly of the 12th century, modified in the 14th and 16th centuries) destroyed by fire in the aftermath of the Civil War. It is thought to have originally been dedicated to St Sithe, but who Sithe was is uncertain. Was she St Sitha, patron saint of housewives? Or was she the martyred Saxon princess St Osyth? In 2000, the church was rededicated as the Church of the Good Shepherd, most fitting for a church in downland country famed for its sheep.

SACRED
TO THE MEMORY
OF
MICHAEL TURNER
CLERK & SEXTON OF THIS PARISH
FOR 50 YEARS
FROM JAN. 17. 1830. TO JAN. 20. 1880.
BORN MAY 25. 1796. DIED DEC. 18. 1885.

HIS DUTY DONE, BENEATH THIS STONE,
OLD MICHAEL LIES AT REST,
HIS RUSTIC RIG, HIS SONG, HIS JIG
WERE EVER OF THE BEST.

WITH NODDING HEAD THE CHOIR HE LED,
THAT NONE SHOULD START TOO SOON
THE SECOND TOO, HE SANG FULL TRUE,
HIS VIOL PLAYED THE TUNE

AND WHEN AT LAST HIS AGE HAD PASSED
ONE HUNDRED – LESS ELEVEN,
WITH FAITHFUL CLING TO FIDDLE STRING,
HE SANG HIMSELF TO HEAVEN.

Warnham

Above: WARNHAM, ST MARGARET'S CHURCH, MICHAEL TURNER'S GRAVESTONE 1927 79582

Right: LULLINGTON, THE CHURCH 1891 28396

Worth

Above: WORTH, ST NICHOLAS'S CHURCH AND THE LYCHGATE
C1960 W146003

Worth Church. An interesting Sussex tradition is that which refers to the north door of churches as the Devil's Door. There are several possible explanations for this: one interpretation is that the north door was where the villagers who were still pagan would enter a church that had been built on an old pagan site, so that they could continue their own practices on a site that still had relevance to them; another tradition was that the north door was left open when a baby was being baptised, so that the departing spirit of the Devil could exit after being commanded to leave the child by the Christian rite. The door would then be hurriedly closed after the ceremony, to prevent the Devil coming back - the churches at Worth (W146003) and Horsted Keynes are particularly associated with this custom. In another tradition, people believed that the Devil waited outside the north door, waiting to catch unwary souls who used it, and that it was quite unsafe to use this exit.

> The association of north doors of churches with the Devil was so strong that most of them have now been blocked up. For instance, the Victoria County History of Sussex entry for the church at Birdham, which has a blocked up north door, describes 'the ancient north door, now blocked, of the same design as the south door, but narrower, and so much lower that it can hardly have had any but a ritual use for the exit of the Devil', and mentions a manuscript dated 1602 which says: 'The north door is clene dammed'.

Above: HYTHE, ST LEONARD'S CHURCH, THE CHARNEL HOUSE 1903   50381A

Hythe

St Leonard's Parish Church. Hythe was once one of the Cinque Ports, and a very busy one, but the sea receded and the quay ended up half a mile inland. St Leonard's Parish Church is set on the hillside above the town. It dates from 1100 and was enlarged in 1165, and the tower was added in 1750; however, most of the church dates from the 13th century. Its most remarkable feature is the magnificent Early English chancel, set higher than the rest of the church and richly embellished with carved mouldings, multiple pier shafts and a stone vaulted ceiling. Here at Hythe and at Rothwell (see photograph on page 83) are the only ossuaries now remaining in England. In the crypt (under the sanctuary) are hundreds of skulls and bones neatly arranged on shelves.

Buried in the churchyard is Lionel Lukin, the inventor of the lifeboat. A bomb dropped in the churchyard of St Leonard's in May 1917 and killed the verger, Daniel Lyth.

Goudhurst

St Mary's Church. This high village of the Weald looks out on a panoramic view of orchards and hopfields, although the foundation of its prosperity in the Middle Ages was based on weaving and iron working. When these declined in the 18th century, they were replaced by smuggling. Near St Mary's is the half-timbered Star and Eagle Inn, which was a centre for this nefarious trade - it is connected to the church by a secret underground passage. The large squat tower of St Mary's was built between 1638 and 1640 at a cost of £750. The top of the tower is 500ft above sea level, and was used as a lookout point in both World Wars. Within the church are wonderful brasses and sculptural memorials to the Culpeper family.

In 1747, the Goudhurst Militia, led by George Sturt, fought a fierce battle with the Hawkhurst Gang of smugglers in the churchyard, while the villagers sought sanctuary within the building's sandstone walls. The gang were driven out of the village, but not without leaving three of their number dead.

Top left: GOUDHURST, THE VILLAGE AND ST MARY'S CHURCH 1901 46378

Below left: GOUDHURST, ST MARY'S CHURCH, THE INTERIOR 1902 48313

Above: WROTHAM, ST GEORGE'S CHURCH 1904   52831

Wrotham

St George's Church. The 13th-century church with its 15th-century tower stands right on the road on the north side of the square. At the foot of the tower, a vaulted passageway extends from north to south beneath it, enabling processions to take place around the west end of the church without leaving consecrated ground. This would otherwise have been impossible, since the adjoining highway abuts the building. Inside the passageway is a stone that may once have held a sanctuary ring granting safety to any alleged criminals who grasped it. The many brasses here form what is almost a portrait gallery: there are fifty figures from five families, dating from 1498 to 1615.

Richard Joy, also known as 'The Kentish Samson', was a local strong man who performed great feats of strength. He died on 18 May 1742, aged 67.

ST PETER'S, (NEAR BROADSTAIRS)
THE GRAVESTONE OF THE KENTISH
SAMSON 1908   60386

Chingford

CHINGFORD, ALL SAINTS' CHURCH 1906 55338

Chingford Church. Built of ragstone, the building is mainly of the 13th century, with a 16th-century brick porch. After a long period of disuse it was restored in 1929. The Frith photograph was taken in 1906, just two years after the nave roof had fallen in. The last service was held in 1889, but the church was never forgotten, and has retained its fame, primarily because of its connections with the Victorian painter Arthur Hughes.

Hughes was born in London in 1830, and was a Pre-Raphaelite painter; he had been influenced by Pre-Raphaelite ideas while he was at art college, and he met Millais in 1852, when they both had paintings entitled 'Ophelia' in the Royal Academy exhibition. His celebrated painting 'Home from the Sea', which shows a boy weeping at his mother's grave, was begun in 1856; true to the realist principles of the Pre-Raphaelites, Hughes painted here in the open air and produced a very accurate portrait of Chingford church and churchyard, but on comparing Hughes's painting and this photograph (which was taken from the same viewpoint as Hughes's painting), it is clear that he has used artistic licence in his positioning of the table tombs and tipsy headstones. In 1863 Hughes added the figure of a girl to the painting, who was modelled by his wife Tryphena Foord.

Harrow-on-the-Hill

St Mary's Church. The poet Byron lived from 1788 to 1824, the son of Captain John Byron and Catherine Gordon. In 1798 he succeeded to the title Baron Byron of Rochdale, and was now able to enjoy an education at Harrow School. He wrote many of his earliest poems lying on John Peachey's tombstone in the churchyard of St Mary's. By nature rebellious and idle, he scorned lessons, and preferred to dream away the hours in solitary contemplation on the Peachey stone. Lord Byron's first collection of poems, 'Hours of Idleness', appeared in 1807. After his tragically early death in Greece, Byron himself was buried in the Byron family vault at Hucknall Torkard Parish Church in Nottinghamshire on 16 July 1824. Permission had been sought for him to be buried at Westminster Abbey, but this was refused.

HARROW-ON-THE-HILL, ST MARY'S CHURCH,
THE PEACHEY TOMB 1906 53636

From 'On a Distant View of the Village and School of Harrow on the Hill'
(from 'Hours of Idleness', 1807)

'Ye scenes of my childhood, whose loved recollection
Embitters the present, compared with the past;
Where science first dawned on the powers of reflection,
And friendships were formed, too romantic to last;

Where fancy yet joys to retrace the resemblance
Of comrades, in friendship and mischief allied;
How welcome to me your ne'er fading remembrance,
Which rests in the bosom, though hope is denied!

Again I revisit the hills where we sported,
The streams where we swam, and the fields where we fought;
The school where, loud warned by the bell, we resorted,
To pore o'er the precepts by pedagogues taught.

Again I behold where for hours I have pondered,
As reclining, at eve, on yon tombstone I lay;
Or round the steep brow of the churchyard I wandered,
To catch the last gleam of the sun's setting ray ...'

Sandhurst

Left: SANDHURST,
ST MICHAEL'S CHURCH
1906 57000

Below: SANDHURST,
ST MICHAEL'S CHURCH,
THE INTERIOR C1955 S56016

St Michael's Church. St Michael's is built in coursed brown rubble with a south-west tower and spire; inside there are wall paintings, but otherwise it is plain and uninspiring, according to Nikolaus Pevsner in his book on Berkshire buildings. The first church on this site dates back to 1220. For 600 years little changed; then in 1853 an energetic new rector began a rebuilding programme. The new south aisle, tower and spire, and east and west ends were designed by G E Street; the design of the Norman-style doorway in the porch entrance of the south-west tower may have been based on an original. The font is Norman in style too, and is said to have been 'executed by one of the daughters of the late rector'. Twelve years later, a new north aisle and the chancel meant that the old church had been completely replaced. Some people may not agree with Pevsner's description of the interior of St Michael's as being 'uninspiring'. The wall paintings (dating from 1880) are striking, and the monuments include a memorial of 1892 in Athenian style to Lady Farrer. A Jacobean brass of 1608 is also worthy of note.

Bisham

All Saints' Church. Bisham's two principal buildings, the church and the abbey, are highlighted by a backdrop of wooded hillsides; they both sit in a charming riverscape. The Norman church's west tower is very close to the Thames and is easily recognised by its single-chamfered bell-openings. The tower arch is round; one respond has a multi-scalloped capital and the other has a waterleaf, dating the tower to around 1170-80. In the north chapel, the reredos includes a late Gothic panel, probably East Anglian, painted with four saints. Much of the church has been restored except the Hoby Chapel, which is typical of the late 16th century.

In the photograph of the Hoby Chapel (23703), the monument nearest the camera is that of Sir Philip Hoby (who died in 1558) and Sir Thomas (1566). The alabaster tomb chest bears the effigies of the two bearded half-brothers wearing their armour, yet relaxed in semi-recumbent poses. Next to them is the tomb of Sir Thomas's widow Elizabeth (she later married Lord Russell), who died in 1609. She kneels in widow's weeds under a canopy with Corinthian columns. Behind her are her deceased children (three daughters and a son), and outside the columns kneel the daughter and two sons who survived her. This tomb is also carved in alabaster. Lady Russell's ghost haunts Bisham Abbey; the story goes that she beat her son to death for blotting his copy book.

Above: BISHAM, ALL SAINTS' CHURCH, THE LYCHGATE 1890   23701P

Below: BISHAM, ALL SAINTS' CHURCH, THE HOBY CHAPEL 1890   23703

Reading

READING, CHRIST CHURCH, THE INTERIOR 1896 37164

Christ Church. Designed by the distinguished architect Henry Woodyer in High Victorian Gothic style, Christ Church was built in 1861-62 and enlarged in 1874. It is large and imposing, with a tower and elegant, distinctive spire 165ft high, a local landmark. Inside, the church is a tour-de-force of Victorian inventive re-interpretation of the medieval Decorated style, with exuberant arcade capitals forming richly foliaged bases for the deeply moulded arches, and unusual reticulated tracery infill to the upper part of the chancel arch. Henry Woodyer obviously enjoyed himself when designing this wonderful church.

Christ Church contains some wonderful Victorian stained glass by renowned artists. John Hardman & Co were responsible for the astonishing east window depicting Christ in Majesty, and Layers, Westlake & Barroud made the large west window. Other windows were created by Clayton & Bell.

Medmenham

Above: MEDMENHAM, THE CHURCH OF ST PETER AND ST PAUL 1890 23712P

Left: MEDMENHAM, THE CHURCH OF ST PETER AND ST PAUL, THE INTERIOR 1890 23713

The Church of St Peter and St Paul.

Halfway between Hambleden and Marlow, on the River Thames, we find the village of Medmenham. Its church stands by the main Henley Road at the north end of the village, at the junction with Ferry Lane which leads south to the river. The ferry is long gone, of course, but the church survives in good heart; it is possible to see it better nowadays, for most of the trees have gone since 1890. The 15th-century tower was re-rendered in 1987, and the roofs retiled soon after, but in 23712p (above) we only get glimpses of the flint and chalk block walls of the church.

The church was heavily restored by the lords of the manor, the Scott-Murrays of nearby Danesfield, most notably in 1839 when the earlier windows were replaced by more 'correct' ones. The woodwork, including the pews, was entirely replaced between then and 1876, apart from the 17th-century roof. During the Second World War a bomb falling nearby destroyed the east window glass we see in 23713 (right). The present window that replaced it is by Christopher Powell. The walls are now more cheerfully whitewashed.

Stoke Poges

St Giles's Church. Situated east of Stoke Park, the medieval church of Stoke Poges is famous beyond its architecture: this is reputedly the churchyard of Thomas Gray's 'Elegy Written in a Country Churchyard', one of the most well-known and well-loved of all English poems.

'The curfew tolls the knell of parting day,
The lowing herd winds slowly o'er the lea,
The ploughman homeward plods his weary way,
And leaves the world to darkness and to me ...

Beneath those rugged elms, that yew-tree's shade,
Where heaves the turf in many a mouldering heap,
Each in his narrow cell for ever laid,
The rude forefathers of the hamlet sleep.'

Gray was buried here in 1777 with his parents near the brick Hastings Chapel of 1558, the left-hand gable in this view. The church underwent considerable change after this photograph was taken, and extensions to the north for a vestry and passageway were added in 1907. The spire, a timber replica built in 1831, was removed in 1924, and there is now a low pyramidal tiled roof in its stead. The creeper has now gone, exposing the Tudor brick of the Hastings Chapel on the left, and no longer is the tower 'ivy-mantled', as Gray described it.

Left: STOKE POGES, ST GILES'S CHURCH AND THE LYCHGATE 1895 35457

South-east of the churchyard, a path through a National Trust-owned copse winds to the fine memorial to Thomas Gray erected by his friend John Penn of Stoke Park in 1799. Designed by James Wyatt, it is a classical sarcophagus on a 20ft-high pedestal. The monument was deliberately designed this high so that it could be clearly seen from Penn's house. Indeed, Penn had the old vicarage demolished and relocated to provide an uninterrupted view. The pedestal panels are, not surprisingly, inscribed with lines from Gray's 'Ode on a Distant Prospect of Eton College' and from his 'Elegy' – 'The paths of glory lead but to the grave'.

Above: HEDSOR, ST NICHOLAS'S CHURCH 1890   23655

Right: HANSLOPE, ST JAMES'S CHURCH C1955   H374009

Hedsor

St Nicholas's Church. Near the Thames on an open chalk ridge overlooking the valley, St Nicholas's Parish Church is set near the Tudor brick and chalk chequered walls of the former manor house, so that the church is in effect the chapel to the big house. The medieval manor house was rebuilt by Rowland Hynd in 1583 – now little remains except the garden walls east of the church. This photograph looks north-west; the church has changed little since 1890. Basically medieval, it was restored in the 1860s when a north aisle and vestries were added. There is a baptistery to the left, behind the hedge, added in 1886. We are looking across to the 18th-century battlemented towers of Lord Boston's Folly, a romantic hilltop eyecatcher in the form of a castle, now converted to a house.

Hanslope

St James's Church. Hanslope is a stone village north-west of Newport Pagnell - it feels more Northamptonshire than Buckinghamshire. St James's Church is one of two churches in the county with a medieval spire (Olney being the other); all the rest are Victorian or later. It was built in 1414, and was originally over 200ft high, but was rebuilt 20ft lower after being struck by lightning in 1804. The church has a late Norman chancel, and in the nave are three of the original stone corbels supporting the roof. These are in the form of angels; one angel plays a horn, one plays a mandore (a plucked stringed instrument), and one holds a shield.

A dreadful tragedy happened in the ringing chamber of the church in 1867. The parish records tell us that 'Joseph James Green from Church End, aged 19, an exemplary Young Man assistant to Mr Fitch, draper was on Friday the 17th May killed while ringing the usual 9.30 am Bell which, not being secured by a stay, turned over and carried poor Green up aloft, and being struck on the head by the beam fell never to recover. He died after a few hours of insensibility. Much Regretted.'

Salisbury

The Church of St Thomas of Canterbury.

The spectacular and atmospheric church of St Thomas of Canterbury stands in the city centre, not far from the cathedral, but hidden away behind a busy city street. As we can see from photograph 19791, it contains a remarkable survival: a complete medieval Doom painting, dating from the 1470s. Christ sits in judgement at the centre, with the blessed on His right hand and the damned to His left; the Devil waits below - and bishops are among those entering the mouth of hell! This amazing painting was whitewashed over in the 1590s and not discovered until 1881, when it was restored.

St Thomas's was originally built in the 13th century for the use of the masons working on the cathedral, and rebuilt in the 15th century by the rich merchants of Salisbury. They created a large, grand church, filled with light from the huge Perpendicular windows in the nave and clerestory. The buttressed south tower was built in four stages from 1400 to 1405. It has Perpendicular bell-openings and panelled battlements. As well as the Doom painting, this church has many other treasures, including the wooden reredos of 1724 by Wren in the south chapel, a 12th-century font, much 14th- and 15th-century stained glass, and a medieval embroidered funeral pall.

Above: SALISBURY, THE CHURCH OF ST THOMAS OF CANTERBURY 1887 19789

Right: SALISBURY, THE CHURCH OF ST THOMAS OF CANTERBURY, THE INTERIOR 1887 19791

*A monument to a keen cricketer,
Nathaniel Hall, in Salisbury cemetery,
Wiltshire carries this epitaph:*

*I Bowl'd, I struck, I stopp'd,
Sure life's a game of cricket,
I blocked with care, with caution popp'd,
Yet death has hit my wicket.*

Above: BEMERTON, ST ANDREW'S CHURCH 1894 34874

St Andrew's Church. The tiny church of St Andrew at Bemerton, on the outskirts of Salisbury, is also known as George Herbert's church. Bemerton's 17th-century rector was the poet George Herbert, who lived in the rectory across the road and is buried in the churchyard. The church, set in a small burial ground with ancient tombs, is alongside a very narrow road blighted by heavy traffic. The church has been over-restored, but a blocked Norman door in the north wall indicates that it dates from the 12th century, and two small windows on the south side are of the Decorated period. Today, the parish church is about three hundred yards away. It is much larger and lavish, and was built by T H Wyatt in 1860-61 for the Pembroke family of Wilton House.

The poet George Herbert was born in Montgomery, Wales in 1593. He was related to the Pembroke family – the Earls of Pembroke live at Wilton House, three miles from Bemerton. Turning his back on high office, he took holy orders in 1630 and retired to Bemerton on the edge of Salisbury. Here he passed the rest of his life as its rector, preaching and writing poetry. He helped pay for the rebuilding of his church, and was a diligent and caring pastoral cleric, beloved of his parishioners - he was nicknamed 'Holy Mr Herbert'. He died of consumption in 1633.

Bromham

Above: BROMHAM, ST NICHOLAS'S CHURCH 1899 44854P

The Irish poet Thomas Moore is buried at Bromham. As well as poetry he penned popular lyrics and songs, including 'The Minstrel Boy' and 'The Last Rose of Summer'. Thomas Moore was a close friend of Lord Byron. One day they were discussing fame and reputation as they strolled alongside the Thames. A boatman began singing one of Moore's songs, and Byron immediately remarked to his friend: 'That is fame.'

The Early English church at Bromham incorporates remnants of its Norman predecessor. It has a central tower and Perpendicular spire, a 14th-century south arcade, and a much restored two-storey Perpendicular south porch. The north windows are also Perpendicular. Nikolaus Pevsner says that the most memorable feature here is the south chapel, the Tocotes and Beauchamp Chapel, later known as the Baynton Chapel. Sir Roger Tocotes and his stepson Sir Richard Beauchamp were given a licence for the chapel in 1492. It has three long bays, and is very ornate, with decorated buttresses and five-light windows with angel busts at their apex. There are monuments here to members of the Tocotes, Beauchamp and Baynton families. William Morris was responsible for the splendid stained glass in the east window, and Constable of Cambridge designed the west window.

Bradford-on-Avon

Above: BRADFORD-ON-AVON, ST LAURENCE'S SAXON CHURCH 1914 66632

Left: BRADFORD-ON-AVON, ST LAURENCE'S SAXON CHURCH 1900 45383

St Laurence's Saxon Church.

This Saxon church had been concealed by sheds and buildings for many centuries. It was rediscovered in the 19th century by Canon W H R Jones, a keen antiquarian; he came across references to it in a text dated 1125. Excavations outside revealed the walls, and repairs revealed the carvings. The simplicity and to some extent the austerity of St Laurence's contrasts with the richness of the churches of later times; we are not used to churches without stained glass, or in fact without windows at all. This church would have been lit by candles. Arthur Mee in his 'King's England' series says about the church: 'It is naked and bare, and all the better for that'. The chancel arch is the narrowest in England at 3ft 6 inches wide. The walls are 2ft 5 inches thick, and the decorations were all cut by Saxon masons. John Chandler and Derek Parker describe the effect of the church on the visitor in 'Wiltshire Churches, an Illustrated History': 'There is an aura of intense mystery, and to submit to its darkness by entering on a sunny day can be a profoundly awesome experience.'

Above: BIBURY, THE CHURCH C1960 B530019

Right: BIBURY, THE SAXON STONE IN THE NORTH SIDE OF THE CHURCH WALL C1960 B530010

Bibury

Bibury Church. At first glance Bibury's church, with its castellated roofline and square tower, looks largely 15th-century. On closer examination, however, the fabric's earlier origins become evident, for inside the church the Saxon chancel arch remains. The church is almost a text-book of architectural history, for the aisles and arcades are Norman, the chancel has Early English lancet windows, and the north aisle windows were inserted in the Decorated period. As we can see from B530019 (above), the churchyard abounds in the tombs of the rich wool merchants who thrived here in the 16th and 17th centuries.

> *Set into the north, or 'Devil's side', of the building is this piece of a Saxon cross shaft with its motif of interlocking rings (B530010), a reminder that the town was once part of the ancient Anglo-Saxon kingdom of Mercia.*

St Andrew's Church. St Andrew's is a late Norman church subsequently augmented during the 14th and 15th centuries by the wealth generated by the local wool trade. The three lower stages of the bell tower are Norman, the upper stage is 13th-century, and the parapet is 15th-century. The most outstanding features are the fine Perpendicular windows on the south side, which were reputedly installed by the Neville family in 1490. To stand in the nave is like being inside a lantern as light floods in through these large windows. Among the church's interesting curiosities are a sundial on the south wall, a stout Norman tub font, and a delicately carved 15th-century pulpit. The belfry contains six bells, all cast by Rudhall's foundry of Gloucester.

Chedworth

Above: CHEDWORTH, ST ANDREW'S CHURCH
C1960   C446015

Left: PAINSWICK, ST MARY'S CHURCH 1900 45597

Above: PAINSWICK, THE LYCHGATE C1955 P3015

Painswick

In September the annual Clipping ceremony takes place in Painswick, as it has done for centuries. It is nothing to do with pruning the trees, but derives from the Saxon word 'clyppan', meaning 'to embrace'. At the ceremony villagers gather in the churchyard, hold hands, and form a circle round the church while singing hymns.

St Mary's Church. Four miles from Stroud, picturesque Painswick is known as 'Queen of the Cotswolds'. At the heart of the village, surrounding the churchyard, stone houses, shops and hotels are gathered, some steeply gabled and half timbered, others Georgian with elegant facades. Above the town, rising to 900ft, is Painswick Beacon with its golf course and Iron Age hill-fort.

The church was built between 1377 and 1399. Its tower houses an impressive peal of 12 bells, and in the nave are an ornamented Tudor tomb and 17th-century font. St Mary's has suffered; it was treated badly in the Civil War (it was besieged by the Royalists, who fired cannons and firebombs into the church to dislodge the Parliamentarians), endured a fire, and was struck by lightning. However, its glory is its beautiful churchyard. Here grow 99 yew trees, planted in the 1790s, now neatly clipped and standing to attention among the picturesque tombs of Painswick's medieval wool merchants, richly carved in glowing Cotswold stone.

Although it looks much older, the lychgate into the churchyard (P3015) was built only a century ago. Its apparent antiquity stems from the fact that its timbers were taken from the former bell frame; a close look at the bargeboards reveals that they are decorated with carved bells.

Deerhurst

The Saxon Church. St Mary's at Deerhurst is one of the finest Saxon churches in Britain, second only in size to Brixworth church in Northamptonshire. The minster of Deerhurst-on-Severn is known to have existed in the early 9th century, and parts of the church may date from that time. After Danish raids the church was rebuilt cAD930, and the nave of the present building is the oldest part still standing. The font is said to be the best-preserved Saxon font in Britain. The tall, thin tower was originally built with two storeys; a third floor was added later, with a triangular-headed window looking down into the nave. The aisles were added around 1200.

Left: DEERHURST, THE SAXON CHURCH 1901   47306

Lying 200 yards south-west of St Mary's, the chapel is a small church built by Earl Odda and dedicated to the Holy Trinity in 1056. It is also thought to be a memorial to Odda's brother Aelfric. The half-timbered building is known as Abbot's Court.

DEERHURST, THE SAXON CHAPEL 1901   47309

Above: SHORTHAMPTON, ALL SAINTS' CHURCH C1955 S830013

All Saints' Church. This plain and simple little church is set close by a farm in the tiny hamlet of Shorthampton near Charlbury. Its origins are Norman, and it has a 13th-century chancel. In the 15th century the nave was widened a shade, but not the chancel. This meant that worshippers were now unable to follow the service. The solution was a squint, cut through the thick wall, allowing people to peer through to the chancel. There are traces of medieval wall paintings, including a Last Judgement and Jonah and the Whale.

    All Saints' Church was furnished during the 18th century with box pews and a high two-decker pulpit with a wig-stand. The chancel was refashioned at the same time, and a new east window was added. The church guide describes the view through the window as 'the loveliest of all altar-pieces, green fields and the good earth'. The porch is a 19th-century addition.

Horley

St Etheldreda's Church. This magnificent wall painting of St Christopher holding the infant Jesus is thought to date from c1450. Painted on the north wall of the church, it was described by Pevsner as being 'one of the most perfect, and largest, representations of the saint in the country.' Where a modern artist might use speech balloons, the medieval artist has used what look like ribbons. St Christopher is asking the boy he carries why he is so heavy, and the boy is replying: 'Yey I be hevy no wonder is for I am ye Kinge of Blys'.

Horley lies on the border with Warwickshire, and its houses are built in the mellow golden local ironstone. So is St Etheldreda's Church; the east end is Norman, and there are lively medieval carvings in the nave arcade. The church was restored by T Lawrence Dale in 1949. He put in a new metal rood and rood screen – the figure of St John on the rood is said to be a portrait of Dale.

Left: HORLEY, ST ETHELDREDA'S CHURCH, THE MURAL OF ST CHRISTOPHER C1955 H234007

In Abbey Dore church there is a memorial to an Elizabeth Lewis who is reputed to have been 141 when she died.

Above: ABBEY DORE, HOLY TRINITY AND ST MARY'S ABBEY CHURCH 1898   41759

Right: ABBEY DORE, THE CHURCH, THE AMBULATORY 1898   41762

Abbey Dore

Abbey Dore Church. The church at Abbey Dore used to be the abbey church for the Cistercian abbey here. The Cistercians were an austere order, and sited their abbeys in remote places; this is certainly an idyllic location amid the beautiful countryside of the Golden Valley. At the Dissolution of the Monasteries in the 1530s, the nave was torn down; what remained was used for a while as farm buildings. Then a hundred years later, Viscount Scudamore restored the building so that it could be used as the parish church – it was re-consecrated in 1634. Thus the church today is the choir, crossing and transepts of the abbey church, all in pure, simple, yet ecstatic Early English style, as we can see from photograph 41762 (right). To this beautiful fabric 'Good Lord Scudamore' added 17th-century fittings – the great oak screen and the stained glass are spectacular, and so is the wooden chancel roof; it is said that 204 Herefordshire oak trees were used to make it.

Above: ROSS-ON-WYE, ST MARY'S CHURCH FROM THE RIVER 1893 32423P

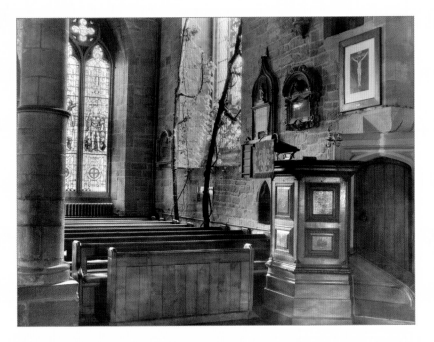

Above left: ROSS-ON-WYE, ST MARY'S CHURCH, THE PULPIT 1938 88647

Above right: ROSS-ON-WYE, ST MARY'S CHURCH, THE CHURCHYARD 1914 67712

> *The 205ft spire of St Mary's had been rebuilt in 1721, when the pinnacles were added – this was mainly paid for through the generosity of John Kyrle, the Man of Ross - but the spire had to be rebuilt in 1852 after being struck by lightning.*

Ross-on-Wye

St Mary's Church. The beautiful town of Ross-on-Wye, perched on its sandstone cliff, is situated in the south-east of the county; its name derives from the Welsh 'rhos', which means a hill or a promontory. The town's setting overlooking the River Wye is quite perfect. St Mary's Church with its slender spire provides a prominent landmark (32423p).

Ross saw a surge in religious activity during the 19th century when many changes were made to the parish church. Major restoration work was carried out between 1862 and 1876. Although there was no evidence remaining of the original Saxon foundation, the Victorians did retain the traces of the Norman structure still to be seen in the chancel, nave and aisles, and also the Markye Chapel of 1510 and the 14th-century tower topped by a slender spire. The interior of St Mary's Church (88647) has seen little change since Frith's photographs were taken. There are numerous monuments including one to John Kyrle, the Man of Ross, another to Elizabeth Markye, many to the Rudhall and Westfaling families, and a macabre one to a town vintner.

Most inhabitants of Ross were buried in St Mary's churchyard (67712). Many of the weathered and leaning tombs commemorate past benefactors, craftsmen, tradesmen, and businessmen who have given their time, energy and money for the improvement of Ross.

> *Apart from the numerous graves with their informative inscriptions, there are other items of interest in St Mary's churchyard, including the Plague Cross, medieval coffin lids, an old stone weight from a church clock, and two handsome stone gateways leading into a garden known as the Prospect, offering an outstanding view of the River Wye's horseshoe bend, Wilton castle and bridge almost hidden by trees, and the rolling hills of Herefordshire and the Welsh borders.*

Above: PEMBRIDGE, ST MARY'S CHURCH C1965 P172025

Pembridge

Tradition has it that the leather on the door of the church is the skin of a marauding Viking, captured on a raid in the area and skinned alive.

St Mary's Church. St Mary's Church is best known for its most unusual detached three-storey belfry, one of seven in Herefordshire, and probably the finest. It dates from the 13th century, and has a stone-built octagonal ground floor, 45ft in diameter, with the upper floors supported on massive oak posts, each of which is a single tree-trunk. There are stone slates on the lower two roofs, and the little spire is shingled. How old is this astonishing building? The local story is that work began on the belfry in 1320, but because of the Black Death, it took forty years to complete. However, information gathered during the belfry's restoration in the 1980s seems to indicate that the timber frame is older, perhaps early 13th-century, and the stone walls date from the 15th and 16th centuries.

Above: QUATFORD, THE CHURCH OF ST MARY MAGDALENE C1960 Q13025

Quatford

Quatford Church. Legend has it that this church was founded by Adeliza, the wife of Roger de Montgomery. Montgomery had come to England with William the Conqueror and been given control of Shropshire. When his wife travelled across the Channel to join him there was a terrible storm. Terrified, Adeliza prayed to God that, should she safely complete her journey, she would build a church at the place where she met her husband. She met her husband under a nearby oak tree (which still survives!) and then built the first church on this site.

Above: SHREWSBURY, ST CHAD'S CHURCH 1911 63233

St Chad's Church. Completed in 1792, St Chad's Church sits on the edge of the old town. It was described in 'Murray's Guide' in 1897 as being in 'execrable taste', and Pevsner only comments on 'its uncommonly beautiful position', but the interior is wonderfully light and airy, with a gallery sitting on cast iron columns – a reminder of the industrial changes taking place locally when it was built. St Chad's is claimed to be the largest round church in England – the main part of the church is completely circular – but this was not the original intention. After the old church collapsed in 1788, an architect called George Steuart was commissioned to design its replacement. He sent in four preliminary ideas for consideration, one in traditional style, and the other three in a circular style. The building committee chose the traditional, and cheapest, design.

Mr Steuart, however, was keen to build a round church, and managed to trick the building committee when they were deciding the exact site of the new church. He sent them a scale plan, which could be fitted over the site plan, so that they could adjust the church's position as they wished, and the committee became so engrossed in deciding the exact spot for the church that they failed to notice that the architect had switched the plan of the church for a circular building. They returned the plans to Mr Steuart with comments on the position but not on the shape of the church, and he went ahead with producing detailed plans for the church as it stands today; when the committee saw the final plans they protested, but were told that this was the design they had 'approved', and that redrawing them to a new design would involve considerable further expense. As the church guide records, 'Reluctant to venture into further expense, and, one imagines, exhausted by months of argument, the committee sullenly agreed to accept Steuart's design'. Views of the church have mellowed with time, and the church literature now claims, with pride, that the church is 'perhaps the finest product of the last phase of the English Renaissance, that is, of the Grecian revival.'

Newport

Newport Church. Originally the word 'port' meant market, so this town's name reminds us that it was a new market town laid out in the early 12th century when Henry I granted the settlement a special charter. Today's buildings still follow the lines of the original burgage plots laid out so long ago.

St Nicholas's Church was named for the patron saint of fishermen. Much of the land locally was very marshy until it was drained in the 18th and 19th centuries, and the numerous pools around the town provided fish both for the local people and a large surplus for sale, so the town's crest includes three fishes as a reminder of where its wealth once came from. The tower of the church dates from the 14th century, but otherwise much of the church was rebuilt in the late 1800s. Inside is a wonderful Arts and Crafts window by William Morris and Edward Burne-Jones that dates from the 1870s.

Charles Dickens visited Newport and heard the story of a local recluse, Elizabeth Parker, who had been jilted on her wedding day. Today the house she lived in has been converted into flats and is known as Havisham Court, after Miss Havisham in 'Great Expectations'.

Top: NEWPORT, ST NICHOLAS'S CHURCH C1960 N26027P

Above: NEWPORT, HIGH STREET AND CHURCH 1893 41982

Tong

Above: TONG, ST BARTHOLOMEW'S CHURCH C1955 T56001

St Bartholomew's is perhaps better known as the place where Little Nell was buried in Charles Dickens's 'The Old Curiosity Shop'. Then, as now, people flocked to visit places where fictional stories took place, and an enterprising churchwarden dedicated an old grave to Little Nell for visitors to see. He even forged an entry in the church's burial register.

St Bartholomew's Church. This is a particularly beautiful church, large and grand, and almost all dating from around 1410. It has come to be known as 'the Westminster of the Midlands'. The church was built by Lady Isabel de Pembrugge to commemorate her family, and the beautiful tombs of the Pembrugges and the Vernons (of Haddon Hall) enrich the church. Many of these are of alabaster, carved with immense artistry. The fan-vaulted Golden Chapel, so called because the glorious vaulting is gilded, was built later, in 1515, as a chantry chapel for Sir Henry Vernon, and it still has remnants of medieval stencilling on the walls. There are also superb bosses, carved misericords, and an epitaph to Sir Thomas Stanley supposedly written by Shakespeare.

Warwick

Amongst the memorials in the chancel of St Mary's Church is one to William Parr, brother of Catherine Parr, Henry VIII's sixth and last wife. William died suddenly in Warwick, and Elizabeth I paid for his funeral.

St Mary's Church. St Mary's Church was badly damaged in the town fire of 1694 - the heat was so intense that it melted the church bells - but fortunately the essentials survived. By 1704 a new nave and a Gothic tower had been built. St Mary's contains one of the most magnificent features of any English church, the incomparable Beauchamp Chapel. Its centrepiece is the tomb of Richard Beauchamp (1382-1439), Earl of Warwick. His effigy lies under a cage-like structure, which at one time supported a velvet or brocade canopy. The earl was undoubtedly concerned for what would happen to his soul after death; the chapel took 21 years to build, and cost over £2,785, probably equivalent to £1,750,000 by today's values. Masses were to be said here for the earl three times a day in an attempt to shorten his time in Purgatory.

Richard Beauchamp, Earl of Warwick, who is entombed in the Beauchamp Chapel of St Mary's Church, oversaw the trial and execution of Joan of Arc; she was burnt at the stake in France in 1430, during the Hundred Years' War.

Above left: WARWICK, ST MARY'S CHURCH 1892 31015

Right: WARWICK, ST MARY'S CHURCH, THE BEAUCHAMP CHAPEL 1892 31021

Above: WILLENHALL, ST GILES'S PARISH CHURCH C1965   W238013

Willenhall

St Giles's Parish Church. Willenhall has changed less than many Black Country towns. It is an industrial town in the Black Country, now in the Metropolitan Borough of Walsall. The medieval church had to be replaced in the 18th century after it had deteriorated. Dr Wilkes, the Willenhall antiquary, tells in his diary that on 6 May 1748 'I set out the foundations of a new church in this town; for the old one being half-timbered, the sills, pillars, etc, were so decayed that the inhabitants when they met together were in great danger of being killed. It appeared to me that the old church must have been rebuilt or at least the middle aisle of it; and that the first fabrick was greatly ornamented'. The new church that Dr Wilkes set out was a plain square building of red brick with a small apse.

In the 1860s a new more sumptuous church was considered desirable. It was built in the fashionable Gothic style, and cost £6,700; it was consecrated by Dr John Lonsdale, Lord Bishop of Lichfield, on 18 July 1867.

The Reverend William Moreton was vicar here from 1795 to 1834. He was addicted to cock fighting, and had his own cockpit at the Church House. He used to preach with the church door open so as not to miss fellow cock fighters passing by on their way to matches at Darlaston Fields - and he would cut short his sermon to follow them.

Wolverhampton

In W285008 St Peter's Church looks out over a busy market day scene next to the Market Hall, built in 1853. In 1961 both the open and closed markets were moved across town to the present site in School Street. All the land in the foreground became a public car park, then the site of the Civic Centre, which was built in 1974.

St Peter's Church. Wolverhampton's parish church was originally dedicated to St Mary and was endowed by Lady Wulfruna in Saxon times. This is how Wolverhampton got its name – it was originally 'Wulfrun Heantun' ('Wulfruna's high town'). The present church was built of sandstone quarried from the rock on which it stands. In medieval times the church, perched up on the ridge, would have been surrounded by a huddle of buildings, and the oldest photographs show that there was a row of medieval buildings in Lichfield Street where the gardens are now. Today there is a building height restriction in force around the church so that it can never be dominated by its neighbours. Thanks to this and to its prominent location the church can be seen from many miles away, especially from the west, when the reddish sandstone of the west front glows from the warm light of the setting sun on summer evenings.

The 9th-century Saxon pillar on the far left of W285503 was carved with intricate animal designs, but a thousand years of weather and pollution have obliterated most of the detail. The tower and nave of St Peter's date from the 15th century. The church was heavily restored in the 19th century, and the incongruous chancel on the right was completely rebuilt in a more sympathetic style.

Above left: WOLVERHAMPTON, ST PETER'S CHURCH
C1955 W285503

Left: WOLVERHAMPTON, THE MARKET AND
ST PETER'S CHURCH 1910 W285008P

In AD910 Tettenhall was the scene of one of the most important battles in English history: it was here that Edward the Elder of Wessex defeated the Danes. The battle marked a turning point. From then onwards the English went over to the offensive, Edward's ultimate aim being the total re-conquest of the Danelaw. The Anglo-Saxon Chronicle tells us: 'This year, the army of the Danes and the English fought at Totanheale on the eighth of the Ides of August, and the English had the victory.'

St Michael's Church. Tettenhall village is two miles from Wolverhampton. St Michael's Church stands on Church Road close to Lower Green. Its predecessor was an important medieval church, but it was almost totally destroyed by fire in 1950 – the story goes that the fire was started by a choir boy smoking! Only the medieval west tower and the Victorian south porch survived. The church was rebuilt by Bernard Miller, who made no attempt to recreate the style of the original.

The old church, according to William White's 'History, Gazetteer and Directory of Staffordshire' (1851), 'was a royal free chapel, and enjoyed all the privileges of such peculiars. It was anciently collegiate. The college was founded previous to the Norman Conquest, and had a dean and five prebendaries, till the period of its dissolution, in the reign of Henry VIII. The present church is supposed to be a part of the original foundation, but it was enlarged in 1825. The font is curiously ornamented with Gothic sculpture, and in the vestry is a venerable oak chest, hewn out of a solid block, and strongly plated with iron.'

Above right: TETTENHALL, ST MICHAEL'S CHURCH
C1965 T140009

Above: TETTENHALL, ST MICHAEL'S CHURCH
C1960 T140013A

Tettenhall

Northampton

Above: NORTHAMPTON, THE CHURCH OF THE HOLY SEPULCHRE FROM THE SOUTH-EAST 1922 72195

Left: NORTHAMPTON, THE CHURCH OF THE HOLY SEPULCHRE, THE INTERIOR 1922 72198

The Church of the Holy Sepulchre. This remarkable church with its circular nave (one of the five surviving in England) dates from the early 12th century. Founded by Simon de Senlis, the crusader Earl of Northampton, soon after 1100 upon his return from the Holy Land, it is based on the plan of the Church of the Holy Sepulchre in Jerusalem. Churches like this were often monastic foundations built by the Knights Templar and the Knights Hospitaller, but this was a private foundation, not a monastic one, and has always been a parish church. The circular nave is next to the tower, but the church was enlarged with a fine 13th-century chancel and later chapels to its east, and a 14th-century tower and spire to its west. The outer walls were much restored by George Gilbert Scott in the 19th century.

Photograph 72198 (left) gives an atmospheric impression of the eight noble Norman columns of the arcade that forms the ring-like aisle of the circular nave. They now support an octagonal clerestory with square-headed windows – this was added in the late 14th century.

Above: EARLS BARTON, ALL SAINTS' CHURCH 1922 72217

Above right: EARLS BARTON, ALL SAINTS' CHURCH, A DOORWAY 1922 72220

Earls Barton

Earls Barton Church. Earls Barton is famous for its church, All Saints', which has a Saxon tower of around AD970. The strip-like stonework on the church is an interesting feature, and was probably intended to resemble the timberwork of an earlier church. Notice too the typical Saxon long-and-short work (alternating perpendicular and horizontal stones) at the quoins of the tower, the small window openings (the ones at the top with baluster pillars, again, typically Saxon), and the plaster rendering, an agreeable contrast to the exposed stone of the rest of the church. This church is one of England's most important Anglo-Saxon monuments.

The tower was built for refuge as well as worship: when the village was attacked by the Danes, villagers would bar the main door of the tower and take refuge higher up, climbing there by a ladder which they pulled up after them. In those dangerous times the church was often the only stone building in the settlement, and so was safe from attack by fire.

Above: ROTHWELL, THE CHARNEL HOUSE IN THE CHURCH CRYPT C1955 R322015

Left: ROTHWELL, THE CHARNEL HOUSE IN THE CHURCH CRYPT C1955 R322016

Rothwell

Rothwell Church. Holy Trinity Church, the longest in the county, has a Norman core, but is mostly now early 13th-century with tall nave arcades with stiff-leaf foliaged capitals. Once larger, it lost the ends of the transepts in 1673 and also various side chapels. Frith's photographer takes us down into the crypt below the south aisle – it was discovered by an 18th-century gravedigger when the aisle floor collapsed beneath him. In it he found a vaulted 13th-century ossuary or charnel house containing the bones from over 1,500 human skeletons removed from the graveyard to make room for new burials. They remain there, neatly stacked.

Leicester

Above: LEICESTER, THE CHURCH OF ST NICHOLAS AND THE JEWRY WALL C1955 L144054

The Church of St Nicholas. The Jewry Wall (see box below) stands next to the superb partly Saxon church of St Nicholas, dating from cAD900. Much Roman masonry and tiles was re-used to build the church – for instance, the arches of the two small Saxon windows on the north wall of the nave are constructed from Roman tiles. The nave is entirely Saxon, and there is some Saxon masonry in the largely Norman chancel. The striking tower with its two rows of blind arcading is also Norman, and so is the north arcade; the south aisle is 13th-century. By the beginning of the 19th century, the church was in a sorry state. The spire was dismantled in 1803, and in 1825 the church itself was threatened with demolition. Luckily for us today, the decision was taken to repair the church instead, and in 1875-76 a new north aisle was built. A splendid new pulpit was installed; copied from an Italian design, it completely encircles a pillar, and its large size gives 'immense scope to more energetic preachers'!

> The remains of Ratae Coritanorum, a regional capital in Roman Britain, and the major local centre for the Coritani tribe, are seen in photograph L144054. This area was excavated by Kathleen Kenyon between 1936 and 1939; at first it was thought that this was the forum and basilica, but the current thinking is that it was a large baths building. The so-called Jewry Wall, 7.3m high, formed part of the palaestra, or exercise hall, to the public baths, dating from about AD130. It is built from Leicestershire and Derbyshire stone bonded with tiles, and it is one of the largest pieces of Roman civilian masonry still standing.

Above: BURTON LAZARS, ST JAMES'S CHURCH C1955 B890057

Burton Lazars

St James's Church. In this village, which is situated two miles from Melton Mowbray, stood the Hospital of St Mary and St Lazarus of Jerusalem, founded by Robert de Mowbray in the mid-12th century – he had probably become acquainted with the Order of St Lazarus of Jerusalem (an Augustinian order) when he participated in the Second Crusade. The ironstone church is also believed to have been founded by Roger de Mowbray. It has a slightly odd appearance with its unusual saddleback double bellcote. The churchyard contains a number of good headstones, including one to Mary Blower of 1781 with a lovely relief of Charity by Christopher Staveley, a Melton Mowbray builder. The spectacular monument seen in the photograph above was erected to weaver William Squire in 1781.

Burton Lazars Hospital was the premier leper colony in medieval England, with a master, eight brothers and leper brethren; the master appears to have been in charge of all the hospitals of the Order of St Lazarus in England. Extensive earthworks on the south-west side of the village mark the site. The emblem of the order was a red cross on a white ground, possibly the origin of the Red Cross organisation's symbol.

Bottesford

St Mary's Church. Tucked away in the far north-eastern corner of Leicestershire in the middle of the magnificent Vale of Belvoir is St Mary's Church, whose spire is the tallest in the county. The best approach to the church is from the south, over a brook and through a group of trees, where there is a delightful view of the 15th-century tower and slender recessed crocketed spire standing over 200ft high. The body of the church is unfortunately rather colourless. However, it is not the architecture that attracts visitors here, but rather the magnificent series of monuments to the Roos family of the 15th century and also to the Manners family, Earls (later Dukes) of Rutland, ranging from 1543 to the 18th century, all crowding the chancel. The monument in photograph 22861 (right) stands in the middle of the chancel, and commemorates the 2nd Earl, who died in 1563. This grandiose table tomb, with no known designer or sculptor, shows the earl and his wife lying under what looks like a dining table, upon which are kneeling figures and a vertical armorial slab. Other tombs here include two by Grinling Gibbons.

Above: BOTTESFORD, ST MARY'S CHURCH, THE EARL OF RUTLAND'S MONUMENT 1890   22861

Above left: BOTTESFORD, ST MARY'S CHURCH 1890   22857

Above right: NEWARK-ON-TRENT, KIRKGATE LOOKING TOWARDS ST MARY'S CHURCH 1900 45106

Above: NEWARK-ON-TRENT, ST MARY'S CHURCH, THE SCREEN 1890 24672

Newark-on-Trent

St Mary's Church. The 252ft spire of St Mary Magdalene towers over the town; St Mary's is a large, grand town church, rebuilt on the site of an earlier church from about 1300 onwards, when a new west tower was begun. Its lower stage is Early English, and above it is built in the Decorated style. Over the following two hundred years or so St Mary's was transformed from a rather plain building into one of the finest parish churches in England. Inside, poppy-head bench ends sweep up to the impressive 16th-century black rood screen (24672, above), the only surviving example of the work of Thomas Drawsword. Beyond, behind the high altar, the gilded reredos looks as though it might date from the 14th century, but it is in fact a masterpiece by Sir Ninian Comper dating from 1937. St Mary's contains a rare survival, two medieval painted panels depicting the Dance of Death.

The timber-framed and jettied building on the left of photograph 45106, now the Charles the First Coffee House, is where Charles's queen, Henrietta Maria, stayed during the Civil War.

Sutton-on-Trent

All Saints' Church. The village lies just off the old Great North Road, whose dual carriageway successor passes it half a mile to the west. All Saints' is one of Nottinghamshire's best parish churches. The wide windows belong to the splendid Mering chapel of about 1525, while the battlemented chancel and nave clerestory are 15th-century. The noble tower is the earliest part of the church – its foundations are Saxon, and the lower part is Norman work, with walls over 4ft thick. Its upper stages are of the 13th and early 14th centuries. There was originally a small spire, which was taken down in 1830. The Mering Chapel was founded by Sir William Mering as a memorial chapel for his family; an old tomb of Purbeck marble is said to be his. All Saints' was sympathetically restored by William Weir of the Society for the Protection of Ancient Buildings in the first years of the 20th century.

Left: SUTTON-ON-TRENT, ALL SAINTS' CHURCH 1913   66080

Edwinstowe

Far left: EDWINSTOWE, ST MARY'S CHURCH C1960 E142018

Left: OLLERTON, THORESBY HALL, THE ROBIN HOOD STATUE C1955 O131039

Vicar of St Mary's from 1884 to 1897 was Dr E Cobham Brewer, who wrote many educational and reference books. Probably the best known of his works is 'Brewer's Dictionary of Phrase and Fable', still in print today; Dr Brewer had published a new and enlarged edition just before he died. He was buried in St Mary's churchyard, and a marble monument marks his grave.

Edwinstowe Church. An Anglo-Saxon settlement grew up here around the chapel on the site of Edwin, King of Northumberland's grave - he had been killed at the Battle of Heathfield in AD633. The present impressive church, dedicated to St Mary, is mostly 12th- and 13th-century. The glorious spire, 140ft high, was added in about 1400; it has been struck by lightning three times, and in the 17th century the church was in a ruinous condition because of the collapse of the spire. The villagers petitioned Charles II to be allowed to fell 200 oak trees from the royal forest to repair the church.

The Sherwood Forest area is, of course, always associated with the deeds of Robin Hood and his Merry Men and their struggles with the Sheriff of Nottingham. Described as 'Robin Hood's village', Edwinstowe lies south of the Sherwood Forest Country Park. It is said that Robin Hood and Maid Marian were married in this church's predecessor by, of course, Friar Tuck.

Above: AMPTHILL, ST ANDREW'S CHURCH C1955   A158011

Ampthill

The first settlement in this central valley was 'Aemethyll' in Old English, which means 'ant-heap' or 'ant-infested hill'. Henry VIII and his court paid many visits to Ampthill Castle, including a final journey in which the king brought his first wife, Katherine of Aragon, to Ampthill for the last years of their married life. It is entirely possible that Queen Katherine worshipped in the church during her stay at Ampthill. The marriage was annulled in 1533 and Katherine was proclaimed Princess Dowager. The castle no longer exists.

Most sources say that Ampthill's parish church dates from the 10th century. St Andrew's most famous monument is a marble memorial to Colonel Richard Nicolls, who captured the Dutch colonial city of New Amsterdam on behalf of the English Crown – and then renamed it New York in honour of his commanding officer, James, Duke of York. The memorial carries a cannon ball in its base; this is said to be the armament that killed Colonel Nicolls during the Battle of Sole Bay in 1672. The roof features twenty 15th-century carved wooden angels, eight with outstretched wings.

There is a Roman column in the chancel of St Andrew's commemorating the Earl of Upper Ossory, who died in 1828. He erected the pump on the market square and Katherine's Cross in Ampthill Park; the cross gained a subsequent measure of recognition in the late 20th century when it proved to be the burial site of the Golden Hare – the subject of a national treasure hunt based on Kit Williams's book 'Masquerade'.

Left: ELSTOW, THE CHURCH
1898 40866

Below: BEDFORD, BUNYAN'S STATUE
1898 40857P

Elstow

Elstow Church. Undoubtedly one of Bedfordshire's most famous sons - if only because of his imprisonment as the result of religious intolerance - John Bunyan was born into a tinsmith's family in Elstow and lived something of the high life before becoming a Nonconformist preacher. In 1660 he was arrested for his beliefs and spent the next 12 years imprisoned in Bedford. Released in 1672 when Charles II issued the Declaration of Religious Indulgence, he was later returned to gaol when the Declaration was rescinded. The significant and most famous outcome of Bunyan's hardships was the writing and publishing in 1678 of a religious parable - 'Pilgrim's Progress'. It became one of the most successful books ever written, being published in over 200 languages. John Bunyan's statue ensures that Bedford's citizens are never far from reminders of 'fire and brimstone' sermons and exhortations to live exemplary lives, and his birthplace of Elstow has become almost a place of pilgrimage.

Bunyan's tribulations and his works are celebrated in the establishment of the 'Bunyan Trail'. This 75-mile-long footpath winds through the Bedfordshire countryside linking elements of Christian's journeys and the more factual aspects of Bunyan's life. Elstow's Norman church, dedicated to St Mary and St Helena, was once the church of a Benedictine nunnery; at the Dissolution all but the nave was demolished, and a new Perpendicular east end was built. Here Bunyan worshipped as a boy, and he rang the bells in the detached bell tower, afraid that the bells would fall down on top of him as punishment for his sins.

Blunham

The Church of St Edmund and St James. St Edmund's stands inside a sizeable walled churchyard to the south-east of the village. It is a sandstone building of the 14th century with an 11th-century tower (restored and partly rebuilt in the 16th century), although the interior fittings include a Saxon font, an indication that an earlier church stood here once.

John Donne, the metaphysical poet, was rector at Blunham from 1621 until his death in 1631 (at this time he was Dean of St Paul's in London as well). The church plate includes a large silver-gilt chalice dated 1626 which was donated by Dr Donne. One of the six tower bells was struck in the 1530s, so Donne would have heard it ring. It might have been hearing this bell that inspired his celebrated line 'Ask not for whom the bell tolls; it tolls for thee.'

Left: BLUNHAM, THE CHURCH OF ST EDMUND AND ST JAMES C1965 B295006

Above left: HITCHIN, ST MARY'S CHURCH 1908 60881

Above: HITCHIN, ST MARY'S CHURCH 1931 84194

Left: HITCHIN, ST MARY'S CHURCH, THE INTERIOR 1901 46647

Hitchin

St Mary's Church. The oldest of Hitchin's churches is St Mary's. It was originally dedicated to St Andrew, and stands in the centre of the town, to the west of the River Hiz. Development over many years has encroached upon the churchyard, which was originally much larger than it is today; burials have turned up as far away as Brand Street.

The existing church dates from the 12th century, reputedly on the site of an earlier Saxon building. Like most of Britain's churches, additions and alterations have been made to it ever since, sometimes by design, and occasionally by necessity: part of the building collapsed in 'a great wind' in 1115, in 1298 more damage was done by an earthquake, and in 1304 the roof fell in. The 13th-century tower (its buttresses are later) has Roman tiles built into it, and a double sundial dated 1660 supplements the clock. The dial is marked 'Anno Salvus', 'the year of salvation', a reference to the restoration of the monarchy following the Civil War. The tower is topped with a short steeple of a type known as a Hertfordshire spike.

In 46647 (left) we look east along the 12th-century nave, the oldest part of the church. Over the chancel arch we can just see an unusual window, which is claimed to be evidence that there was once a central tower. The font (foreground) has been in the church since at least 1470 (the remarkable font cover is Victorian). It is carved with twelve apostles, whose faces were hacked off by Puritan soldiers in the 17th century.

Iron railings (see 60881, above left) once surrounded the churchyard to keep out the resurrection men, or bodysnatchers, who stole corpses for dissection by the medical profession. The railings were erected by public subscription following the theft of the body of Elizabeth Whitehead in 1828; Elizabeth was not the first victim, but the townsfolk were resolved that she should be the last. The railings were removed before the Second World War, and not during it as is sometimes suggested. The burial ground surrounding St Mary's contains gravestones bearing a skull and crossbones motif. Some say that these memorials mark the last resting place of either plague victims or pirates, but neither explanation is true. This gruesome depiction of death was fashionable in the late 17th century, and can be found in many churchyards in England.

Bengeo

St Leonard's Church. St Leonard's Church at Bengeo, said to be the oldest building in the Hertford area, dates from the 12th century. It appears to have been built in 1120 to replace a wooden church, which was probably destroyed by the Danes. It is built of flint with stone dressings, and it has a fine semicircular apsidal east end, whose tiny east window is original; some of the other windows were inserted later. On the north side of the chancel are two openings through the wall concealed by sliding panelling; one was probably a cupboard, but the other is thought to have been cut so that an anchorite could gain access to the church from his or her cell. Some faint traces of wall paintings remain.

This beautiful example of Norman architecture fell into a derelict state, and an inappropriate gabled roof had been built over the chancel by the 19th century. The church of Holy Trinity in New Road, consecrated in June 1855, took over as the place of regular worship. Fortunately St Leonard's was later restored both externally and internally.

Left: BENGEO, ST LEONARD'S CHURCH 1922 71877

Above: BENGEO, ST LEONARD'S CHURCH 1929 81779

Much Hadham

Above: MUCH HADHAM, THE VILLAGE AND
ST ANDREW'S CHURCH FROM BUSH HILL 1899 44879

Some of the windows in St Andrew's were designed by
the sculptor and artist Henry Moore, who lived at nearby
Hoglands in Perry Green.

St Andrews Church. Little has changed in the 100 years since this photograph was taken. On the left, peeping through the trees, are the white gables of the Old Rectory, and in the foreground are the meadows skirting the River Ash which were part of the grounds of the Bishop of London's palace just out of the view to the right. This view was taken from the east, and shows the fine tracery of the church window and the traditional Hertfordshire spike on the tower. St Andrew's was originally built in the 12th century, and was rebuilt and altered over the years, culminating in the tower of c1380, which was added by Bishop Braybrook. In the 15th century the clerestory and the roof were renewed – the roof is very fine, and has hardly changed since it was built.

East Horndon

All Saints' Church. This idiosyncratic red brick church, set in a prominent position on top of a hill, was built in the late 15th and early 16th centuries, mainly thanks to the Tyrell family; they are responsible for the unusual upper rooms in the transepts which form small galleries, and for the Tyrell chantry chapel containing their memorials. These include a limestone portrait slab of Alice Tyrell dated 1422. The church suffered from neglect and vandalism until being rescued by volunteers in 1970. Note the prominent wooden 'headboard' grave in this photograph: these are fairly scarce in Essex.

The Church of St George and St Gregory. Pentlow lies between Sudbury and Cavendish. A remarkable monument was erected here in 1859 by the Rev Edward Bull in memory of his father. It stands in the grounds of the rectory, a 90ft-tall octagonal red brick tower, tapering slightly from a base 16ft in diameter. It is said that from the top it is possible to see 40 churches. These include Pentlow's church, of course, which forms a sort of frontier post: Pentlow is the northernmost parish in this part of Essex.

The church dates from the 12th century, and was altered in the 14th century, when the tower, one of only six round towers in the county, was built – its walls are 4ft thick. The rest of the church is basically 12th-century, including the beautiful semi-circular apse at the east end. Inside is a massive square Norman font decorated with carvings of stars, rings and foliage and a beautifully carved font cover of the 15th century.

Pentlow

Above: EAST HORNDON, ALL SAINTS' CHURCH 1907 57588

Right: PENTLOW, THE CHURCH OF ST GEORGE AND ST GREGORY 1904 51176

In the north chapel of the Church of St George and St Gregory is a splendid monument to Judge George Kempe, who died in 1606, his wife, and one of his sons; the monument also depicts four more sons and ten daughters!

Another earthquake was to hit Colchester after the tremor of 1692 described below - the Great Colchester Earthquake of 22 April 1884. This earthquake, which is said to have measured 6.9 on the Richter Scale, was estimated to have destroyed 1,200 buildings in the area of Colchester and the surrounding villages, and many churches were damaged.

Left: COLCHESTER, ST PETER'S CHURCH 1907 57543

St Peter's Church. There was probably a church here in Saxon times, because St Peter's is mentioned by name in the Domesday Book, and is said at this time to have two priests – it must, therefore, have been well established. Later records show that it was richly endowed by the early 14th century, and at that time it had a central tower. In the 15th century the north and south aisles were built. By this time Colchester was a prosperous town thanks to the cloth industry, and the remarkably large number of memorials and particularly brasses in St Peter's show that many rich merchants worshipped here. In 1692 the old central tower was shaken by an earthquake. This event was recorded by an eyewitness in the Register of St Peter's:

'... on Thursday Sept: 8 1692 there happened about two of ye Clock in the afternoon for ye space of a minute or more an universall earthquake all over England France Holland & fome parts of Germany. and particularly it waf attefted to me by the Masons that were then a plaistring the Steeple of St Peter in this Towne & upon the upper most scaffold that the steeple parted fo wide in ye midst that they could have put their hand into the crack or cleft y immediately shut up clofe again, without any damage to the workmen (who expected all would have fallen down) or to the fteeple it felf, most of the houfes here and elfewhere fhooke, & part of a chimny fell downe on North Hill, & very many who were fenfible of it were taken at ye same time with a giddynef in their head, for fom fhort time, in witnefs of wt is here related I have here fet my hand.'

ROBERT DICKMAN, MINISTER OF ST PETER'S, COLCHESTER

In 1758 the shaky tower was demolished and a new one built at the west end, a typically dignified Georgian design in red brick with stone quoins. At this time, too, the attractive panelled galleries were added; the fact that they have never been removed indicates the continuing importance and popularity of this church.

Little Maplestead

Above: LITTLE MAPLESTEAD, THE CHURCH OF ST JOHN THE BAPTIST C1955 L157002

The Church of St John the Baptist. The village of Little Maplestead was granted to the Knights Hospitaller by Juliana Dosnel in the 12th century, and in about 1340 the Knights Hospitaller built this church. They modelled it on the plan of the church of the Holy Sepulchre at Jerusalem: that is, it is circular, discounting the chancel and porch. There are only four other churches of this sort in England. Dividing the circular space into a hexagonal 'nave' and circular 'aisle' is a 14th-century arcade, and the seats in the chancel have room for two people each. The circular part of the church is topped by a wooden belfry. When the order of the Knights Hospitaller was dissolved at the Dissolution, this building became the parish church. In the 1850s the church underwent a drastic restoration – the exterior of the walls, the windows, and the furnishings are Victorian.

The Knights Hospitaller were a military monastic order, called in full the Order of the Hospital of St John of Jerusalem. The order was founded in the 11th century to give military protection and hospital care to pilgrims to the Holy Land during the crusades.

Aldeburgh

GEORGE CRABBE

Aldeburgh Church. The sacrifice made by seven brave seamen is commemorated by the simple but striking memorial we see in photograph 50439. In 1899 the lifeboat 'Aldeburgh' foundered in heavy seas. A local appeal raised funds for the dependants and for the construction of the monument. There is a justifiable pride in being a lifeboatman, and in photograph 50426 coxwain James Cable and his men proudly show off the 'City of Winchester', presented by that city, a replacement for the 'Aldeburgh' so tragically lost a few years before. This boat served until 1928 and saved forty lives.

Aldeburgh church, dedicated to St Peter and St Paul (50439), will have heard many prayers for seamen and lifeboatmen. Its flint tower looks out to sea, and inside the church is a memorial to George Crabbe, rector of Aldeburgh and its celebrant in verse – his long poem 'The Borough' (1810) tells of a seaside town and its people, including the fisherman Peter Grimes. Peter Grimes was the subject of an opera by Aldeburgh's most famous resident, the composer Benjamin Britten; he is commemorated by a splendid stained glass window by John Piper and Patrick Reyntiens.

Top: ALDEBURGH, THE LIFEBOATMEN'S MEMORIAL 1903 50439

Above: ALDEBURGH, THE LIFEBOAT 'CITY OF WINCHESTER' 1903 50426

While most people imagine lifeboats generally to be launched from slipways, Aldeburgh lifeboats such as the 'City of Winchester' have always been launched straight from the shingle beach; the crew had to row her through the heavy surf until they could manage to raise the sails, and then still find the strength to carry out the rescue. In 1881 the Aldeburgh boat had to stay at sea in a dreadful snowstorm for almost thirty hours, having sailed a total of 120 miles.

Above: BLYTHBURGH, THE CHURCH OF THE HOLY TRINITY 1891 28357

Blythburgh

Blythburgh was quite an important place in bygone times, and was once a thriving port. In the same way as many other river ports, it lost trade when its waterways could no longer cope with the increasing draughts of cargo ships. The church, known locally as 'the cathedral of the marshes', presents an imposing landmark set on high ground above the River Blyth. It was entirely rebuilt in the mid to late 15th century, on a massive scale, 128ft long with a tower 83ft high - this had a spire until 1577. The church was over-sized and over-opulent for an area dependent on small-scale farming and a little fishing. Physical decline began as early as the 16th century, and accelerated through periods of poverty, damage and indifference. The gentle ministrations of 20th-century restorers have created an ambience of stunning brightness and simplicity. The large windows bring light and awe to the interior, and the glorious painted angels soar above on the roof-beams.

Stranger, pass by and waste no time
On bad biography and careless rhyme.
For what I am, this humble dust encloses;
And what I was is no affair of yourses.

Suffolk, 1870

Bramfield

St Andrew's Church. This is the only church in East Anglia to have a detached Norman round tower. Was it originally built for defensive purposes? St Andrew's is a charming church, built in the Decorated period, and unusual in that it has a thatched roof. Inside, the rood screen remains, perhaps the best example in Suffolk, still with paintings of saints, and delicate miniature hovering angels under the vaulted loft. There is a faded wall painting of the Holy Rood on the north wall.

St Andrew's contains two remarkable monuments. One is the masterpiece of the 17th-century sculptor Nicholas Stone, a moving alabaster effigy of Elizabeth Coke, who died in childbirth. The other is the monument to Bridgett Applewhaite; the long epitaph records how she died in 1737 on the eve of her second marriage. '...After the Fatigues of a Married Life, Born by her with Incredible Patience, ... And after the Enjoiment of the Glorious Freedom Of an Easy and Unblemisht Widowhood, ... She Resolved to run the Risk of a Second Marriage-Bed, But DEATH forbad the Banns. And having with an Apoplectick Dart Toucht the most Vital part of her Brain; ... In Terrible Convulsions Plaintive Groans, or Stupefying Sleep, Without Recovery of her Speech, or Senses, She Dyed ...'

Rickinghall Inferior

Rickinghall Inferior Church. Rickinghall Inferior (so called because the village lies physically lower than its neighbour Rickinghall Superior) is situated in rolling farmland between Bury and Diss. This area has a long history: there was an Iron Age settlement close by, and a Romano-British pottery kiln was found in the village. The Norman round tower of flint-built St Mary's Church was extended in the 14th century into a charming octagonal top with battlements; recent repairs have shown that there is an earlier tower beneath the outer skin of flints. The 14th-century porch was later heightened to form an upper room, hence the small low windows on the ground floor. The tall monument on the right of the photograph is to Lieutenant Richard Maul, who died in 1874. The nave of St Mary's is probably originally Norman, but it was much altered in the 13th and 15th centuries – the only Norman feature remaining inside the church is the tower arch. St Mary's has a beautiful 14th-century south aisle – one of the windows here has exceptionally fine geometrical tracery.

Top: BRAMFIELD, ST ANDREW'S CHURCH C1960 B878003

Above: RICKINGHALL INFERIOR, ST MARY'S CHURCH C1965 R327005

Woolpit

St Mary's Church. This spectacular example of medieval architecture is a double hammer-beam roof, an exclusively East Anglian structure, of which Suffolk has two-thirds of the total. There are 106 angels on the hammers, wall plate and wall posts, all hovering with outstretched wings over the congregation at worship. There are yet more angels in the aisle roofs, flying head to head on the rafters. There is another amazing spectacle over the chancel arch. This is a canopy of honour, a vaulted canopy that once covered the rood; the beautiful lierne vault meets the easternmost hammer-beams of the roof, forming a most satisfying and harmonious design. As if this was not enough, the entrance to St Mary's is a grand two-storey porch adorned with niches in front and a pierced parapet above.

The name of the village is not derived from the wool industry, but from wolves – legend says that there was once a pit here to trap them.

Left: WOOLPIT, THE CARVED ROOF OF ST MARY'S CHURCH C1955 W442011

Ranworth

St Helen's Church. St Helen's, one of the most beautiful of the many lovely Broads churches, and known as 'the cathedral of the Broads', stands a short walk from the staithe. The road has widened little since 1934; the owners of the old-fashioned bicycles propped against the fence (86390, right) are working on the verge opposite.

The glory of St Helen's is the mid 15th-century rood screen (86391), considered by many to be the finest in the country – it luckily escaped damage by Cromwell's troops. It is complete with its loft, and still retains its original painting; the panels contain beautifully-coloured portraits of apostles and saints, medieval masterpieces. The font and 15th-century lectern are both noteworthy, and a medieval antiphoner (an illuminated book of church music) in superb condition is on display. If you feel energetic, a climb to the roof of the tower will reward you with a magnificent view over broadland.

Above: RANWORTH, ST HELEN'S CHURCH 1934 86390

Left: RANWORTH, ST HELEN'S CHURCH, THE ROOD SCREEN 1934 86391

On Mr Partridge
What! Kill a partridge in the month of May!
Was that done like a sportsman? Eh, Death, eh?

Norfolk, 1861

Cawston

Above: CAWSTON, ST AGNES'S CHURCH C1965 C415012

Above right: CAWSTON, ST AGNES'S CHURCH, THE INTERIOR C1965 C415013

St Agnes's Church. In its heyday this was a huge village with shops of every description and five prosperous inns. The fine church has a tower 120ft high; it is famous for its hammer-beam roof adorned with carved angels and its fine rood-screen, unusually tall, and painted with images of the saints. These saints include Good Sir John Schorne, a 14th-century rector, water diviner, and discoverer of a cure for gout, which made him so famous that he was numbered among the saints! The pulpit once had a large leather funnel with a pipe going down to a pew for a particularly deaf member of the congregation.

'God spede the plow and send us ale corn enow our purpose to make: at crow of cok of the plowlete of Sygate: be merry and glede war good ale yis work mad'. This inscription, on the balustrade of the tower gallery, bears testament to Cawston's agricultural origins. Ale corn is barley, and the inscription relates to a celebration held by the Plough Guild of Sygate for the raising of funds.

Booton

Above: BOOTON, ST MICHAEL AND ALL ANGELS' CHURCH C1960 B539002A

St Michael and All Angels' Church. 'Perhaps the most enthralling ecclesiological curiosity in Norfolk.' So said the Rev C L S Linnell in the 'Collins Guide to English Parish Churches' (1958). This is indeed a singular and quirky building; the Rev Whitwell Elwin, an amateur architect, designed the church, which was built between 1875 and 1900 using the walls of the original medieval church, encasing them with typical Norfolk split flint work. The architect and builders clearly enjoyed themselves: crockets, finials and even a minaret jostle for space with the two triangular western towers to make a dazzling feast for the eyes. Inside there is a hammer-beam roof with angels. These, which have been described appositely as 'muscular', project forward to an almost alarming degree – it is not surprising that they were made by a carver of figureheads for ships.

East Dereham

St Nicholas's Church. In photograph 33308p we see a quiet lane on the fringes of this town, which sits at the centre of the county. In the background are the two towers of St Nicholas's Church – the second detached bell tower was built in the churchyard in the 15th century, presumably because the existing tower was not strong enough for bells (33305). St Nicholas's has a Norman south doorway and a celebrated panelled font of 1468 which cost £12 13s 9d. This is a rare survival, for it depicts the Seven Sacraments – fonts like this were usually destroyed by the Puritans, who objected to the idea of more than one sacrament. (The Seven Sacraments are Mass, Ordination, Matrimony, Extreme Unction, Baptism, Confirmation and Penance.) The poet William Cowper, 'England's sweetest and most pious bard', and a gentle, troubled man, was laid to rest here. He died in 1800, and his monument (46548, below) is by Flaxman.

In the early 19th century, the bell-tower of St Nicholas's was used to house French prisoners of war: one, shot while trying to escape, is buried in the adjoining churchyard.

Top left: EAST DEREHAM, ST NICHOLAS'S CHURCH 1893 33308P

Above left: EAST DEREHAM, ST NICHOLAS'S CHURCH 1893 33305

Above: EAST DEREHAM, ST NICHOLAS'S CHURCH, THE COWPER MONUMENT 1901 46548

Above: GRANTCHESTER, THE CHURCH OF ST ANDREW AND ST MARY 1929 81771

Grantchester Church. Grantchester lies in meadows beside the River Cam, a few miles from Cambridge, and the last two lines of Rupert Brooke's poem, 'The Old Vicarage, Grantchester', have immortalised the church:

'Stands the church clock at ten to three -
And is there honey still for tea?'

It is believed that the clock was actually broken when the poet was living in Grantchester. For years after Brooke's death in the First World War, the clock was kept at that time as a memorial to him.

The church is dedicated to St Andrew and St Mary. The nave is 15th-century, with a south aisle built during a major restoration in 1876-77. The chancel is older than the nave, built in the Decorated style; the side windows have flowing tracery, and are separated by niches with carved canopies over them which would once have contained statues of the saints. The tower was built around 1420, and was repaired at various times over the years. The clock made famous by Rupert Brooke was put up in the 1870s. There are three bells, which date from the 17th century; the frame from which they hang, and the floor of the ringing chamber, are made from oak hewn in the Middle Ages.

St Ives

The Parish Church of All Saints. St Ives was first known as Slepe, an Anglo-Saxon word meaning 'muddy' – very suitable for a town on the edge of the Great Fen! It became St Ives in the early 11th century after a farmer ploughed up a stone coffin containing the body of St Ivo. A priory was founded, and it became a place of pilgrimage.

There has probably been a church on this site since Saxon times; the present building dates from the 12th century, but it was largely rebuilt between 1450 and 1470. The noble spire is set behind a battlemented and pinnacled parapet. Inside there is a 13th-century font (41285, foreground left), an Elizabethan pulpit and a vast organ built in 1893. The spire has been particularly accident-prone. In 1741, it was blown down, and was rebuilt in 1748. A second rebuilding took place in 1879 - this is the spire we see in the photograph. Then, on 23 March 1918, an aircraft from the RAF (previously the RFC) station at Wyton landed in a nearby water meadow to ask some local lads the way back to the airfield. Shortly after taking off again, it veered sharply and clipped the top thirty or so feet from the top of the spire; aircraft and pilot fell into the church, and the pilot was killed instantly. The damaged section of the spire was renewed in 1924.

Above: ST IVES, THE PARISH CHURCH OF ALL SAINTS, THE INTERIOR 1898 41285

Right: ST IVES, THE PARISH CHURCH OF ALL SAINTS 1899 44251

Castor

Above: CASTOR, THE CHURCH OF ST KYNEBURGHA 1890 24457

Legend has it that Kyneburgha, while on a mission of mercy, was chased by three wicked men who wanted to attack her. However, a huge trench opened up behind her, and the men were buried – thus her honour was preserved. During the chase, she had dropped her basket; from it grew a carpet of flowers. The capital of one of the pillars in the church is carved with two fighting men and a fleeing maiden – is this a depiction of Kyneburgha's escape?

The Church of St Kyneburgha. To the west of Castor lies Ermine Street, a Roman road; excavations have shown that the village is built over a large Roman estate. About 200 years after the departure of the Romans from Britain, Kyneburgha founded a convent here in AD650. Parts of the Saxon church are incorporated into the cruciform church, the most important Norman church in Cambridgeshire. The church, dedicated in 1124 to St Kyneburgha, the third of four daughters of Paeda, King of Mercia and founder of the abbey at Peterborough, stands on a slight rise overlooking the village and the River Nene. The striking Norman tower is decorated by window openings that are repeated as blind arcades; the spire was added in the 14th century. Inside, the roofs of the nave, aisles, south porch and priest's room are thickly adorned with carvings of angels, many of them playing musical instruments.

Top left: STAMFORD, ST MARY'S CHURCH C1955 S177060

Top right: STAMFORD, ST MARY'S CHURCH, THE WEST DOOR 1922 72330

Above: BOSTON, ST BOTOLPH'S CHURCH, THE NAVE LOOKING EAST 1890 26075

Stamford

St Mary's Church. St Mary's Church is the most eye-catching of Stamford's churches, with a broach spire rising to 163ft. The spire dates from the early 14th century, one hundred years later than the tower on which it stands. Inside, the church gives the impression of being almost square, with the chancel hidden behind J D Sedding's 1890 rood screen. It is topped by a cross designed by Harold Bailey, and it was dedicated as a war memorial in 1920. The north chapel has a particularly fine blue and gold-embossed ceiling, and some spectacular stained glass by Christopher Whall, an Arts and Crafts artist. The west door, tower and spire of St Mary's hold a wealth of architectural detail, with blind arcading, niches holding statues of the four Evangelists, and elaborate openings in the spire.

Boston

St Botolph's Church. Boston, Botolph's Town, was laid out along the banks of the River Witham some time around 1100 within the parish of nearby Skirbeck, and rapidly became a great port, although it only received its first charter in 1205 from King John. It acquired town walls in 1285, and in 1353 it wrested away Lincoln's wool staple. It was the wool trade that built the town with its seething market and vast numbers of ships.

The town centre is dominated by its very large triangular market place which in its turn is visually overwhelmed by the mighty church tower, completed in the 16th century and universally known as the Boston Stump. Crowned by a superb octagonal lantern complete with pinnacles and flying buttresses, it soars 272ft above the town and can be seen from miles around, even from Lincoln; it served as a landmark for shipping, for the lantern used to have a beacon lit in it at night.

The noble interior of St Botolph's is as overwhelming as its exterior. It is a magnificent example of the Decorated period, with the dignified nave arcades and vaulted roof leading the eye to the soaring chancel arch and the vast east window. In the chancel the original 14th-century choir stalls survive, along with 62 wonderful misericords; the carvings include a monk thrashing a boy, a bear playing an organ, a mermaid and sailors, and a virgin and a unicorn.

BOSTON, THE RIVER AND ST BOTOLPH'S CHURCH 1893   32062P

Grantham

St Wulfram's Church. St Wulfram's Church is an example of English Gothic at its most magnificent. The west front, which includes the tower and spire, was started in c1280; at nearly 283ft high, it was at that time the highest spire ever built. As the pioneer, it was probably the model for those higher ones that were built later. But it is the design of the tower rather than its height that matters. The slight tapering of the tower, the pinnacles that mediate between tower and spire, the mouldings on the spire's partitions – all these things contribute to a wonderful whole, a spectacle that is said to have made Ruskin faint the first time he saw it. The prospect we see in 22277 no longer exists – trees planted in 1916 now block the view.

Grantham is mentioned in the Domesday Survey of 1086, when it had one church, four watermills and a population of about 1,300. Thus there was probably a Saxon church here, but the oldest parts of the present-day church are the clustered Norman columns of the mid 12th century along the nave (22279) - that is, if we ignore what appears to be some Anglo-Saxon herring-bone stonework by the side of the organ case. This could have been part of the original Saxon church, possibly its tower.

The south porch contains another of Grantham's great treasures, the chained library (22285). It was founded in 1598 by the Rev Francis Trigge, the rector of the nearby Lincolnshire village of Welbourn. The library was catalogued in 1988, and a total of 82 chained books were repaired and restored. The earliest is one of 1472, which is bound with two others dated 1476.

Top left: GRANTHAM, ST WULFRAM'S CHURCH 1889 22277

Below left: GRANTHAM, ST WULFRAM'S CHURCH, THE NAVE LOOKING EAST 1889 22279

Below right: GRANTHAM, ST WULFRAM'S CHURCH, THE CHAINED LIBRARY 1889 22285

Wallasey

Above: WALLASEY, THE CHURCH AND THE TOWER C1873 8468

On the south wall of St John's Church is a monument to Diana Warburton. It is unusual in that she is shown as a skeleton holding her winding sheet, upon which is written her obituary.

Wallasey Church. The old Wirral village of Wallasey has developed slowly. The Wirral was colonised by the Norsemen long ago, and many names reflect those invaders who settled here. St Hilary's is the old parish church of Wallasey. There are not many churches dedicated to this saint, and this particular church is unique because of its two towers. There has been a church on this site for over a thousand years. Twice a fire has destroyed the buildings: the lone tower dates from a church built c1530 which caught fire in the 1850s. The tower was saved, and the new church, seen behind, was built slightly away from the old tower. The older tower is noted for its gargoyles.

Though fishing was the principal industry of the village of Wallasey, James Stonehouse, who knew the area in the late 17th century, portrayed the inhabitants as a shifty lot who made their real livings through less legal means. He wrote that 'the inhabitants were nearly all wreckers and smugglers – they ostensibly carried on the trade and calling of fishermen, farm-labourers and small farmers; but … many a fierce fire has been lighted on the Wirral shore on stormy nights to lure the good ships on the Burbo or Hoyle Banks. There is scarcely a house in the north Wirral that could not provide a guest with a good stiff glass of brandy or Hollands.' Perhaps that explains why once, when St Hilary's Church burnt down, it was said that the flames had the blue haze of burning brandy!

Daresbury

Above: DARESBURY, ALL SAINTS' CHURCH C1955 D151002

In the Daniell Chapel of Daresbury church is the Lewis Carroll Memorial Window, funded by Lewis Carroll fans from all over the world to commemorate the centenary of his birth – it was completed in 1935. Designed by Geoffrey Webb (he had worked with the renowned stained-glass artist C E Kempe), this remarkable window shows a Nativity scene surrounded by panels symbolising Carroll's life and depicting characters from the Alice books.

All Saints' Church. There has been a church here since the 12th century, but the present building dates from 1870. The tower is 16th-century, and so is the oak pulpit, richly carved with angels and grotesques, and also the rood screen, adapted in Victorian times to make a partition between nave and chancel and the panelling behind the altar; it too is richly carved, with one panel depicting a green man. In the tower is a peal of eight bells, and a rhyme to the bellringers dated 1730.

The church is most famous for its association with Charles Lutwidge Dodgson, better known as Lewis Carroll, author of 'Alice's Adventures in Wonderland', 'Through the Looking Glass', and much more. He was born and baptised here in 1832, for his father was Vicar of Daresbury, and many of the characters that feature in his books are thought to have been inspired by the strange carvings within the church. He had a happy boyhood here – he later wrote of Daresbury as:
'An island farm, mid seas of corn,
Swayed by the wandering breath of morn,
The happy spot where I was born.'

Farndon

Above: FARNDON, ST CHAD'S CHURCH C1960 F161002

St Chad's Church.

Farndon lies seven miles south of Chester. There are some 16th-century houses here, and the famous 16th-century map-maker John Speed was born in this village. During the Civil War a battle was fought here for control of the strategic bridge over the Dee leading to Wales, and in St Chad's Church there is a rare and highly interesting stained-glass memorial window to the Royalists. It was made in 1662, and shows in fascinating detail soldiers, armour, and equipment, along with Sir Francis Gamul (the Royalist colonel), and the composer William Lawes, personal musician to Charles I, killed at the battle of Rowton Moor, Chester. An ancient yew stands in the churchyard, and it is said that the Civil War soldiers leant their weapons against it.

> St Chad's is one of the few churches that still carries out a rush-bearing ceremony each year: fresh rushes are brought into the church, and also laid on the paths and graves outside. This recalls a time when churches still had mud floors, which would have been covered with rushes to provide a dry footing for the congregation.

JOHN SPEED

Nether Alderley

Above: NETHER ALDERLEY, THE CHURCH
AND THE RECTORY 1896 37474

Right: NETHER ALDERLEY, THE STAIRS TO
THE STANLEY PEW, ST MARY'S CHURCH
2005 N148705K

St Mary's Church. The 14th-century St Mary's Church at Nether Alderley has a strange pew perched up on the wall, built by Thomas Stanley, the area's greatest landowner. He wanted to demonstrate his position in the parish, so he built a private pew for himself in the church. Elevated above the nave like a Jacobean opera box, it has to be reached by an outside stair, shown in photograph N148705k. Once it would have had a direct view of the pulpit, which used to be further west than it is now. The design also reflects the religious changes of the Reformation. Families of the gentry no longer built their private chapels with a priest to say masses for their souls. They needed comfortable seating to listen to the long sermons that were such a feature of 17th-century religious life.

St Mary's contains a precious book, a Breeches Bible that dates from 1560. Breeches Bibles were so named because of the translation of the story of Adam and Eve covering themselves with fig leaves: 'They sewed fig leaves and made themselves breeches'.

Marton

Above: MARTON, THE PARISH CHURCH OF ST JAMES AND ST PAUL 1897 40468

The Parish Church of St James and St Paul. Marton lies 25 miles south of Manchester. It is the home of Cheshire's oldest oak tree, said to be 600 years old. Despite the brickwork at the east end, Marton's black and white church of St James and St Paul is even older than the tree. It is the oldest surviving timber-framed church in Europe still in use – it was founded in 1343 by Sir John de Davenport. It stands on a man-made mound; is this a prehistoric site? Internally the church is quite delightful; it even has the remnants of an early medieval wall painting on the west wall depicting the Last Judgment.

Ashbourne

Ashbourne Church. Once famously described by the novelist George Eliot as 'the finest mere parish church in England', St Oswald's has long been regarded as one of Derbyshire's best churches. Its setting is most attractive, and the visitor enters through fine wrought-iron gates, dating from 1700 and decorated with skulls and flames. The church has an unusually long Early English chancel, and aisled transepts; over all soars the massive yet graceful 212ft spire. Inside St Oswald's there is a feast of carvings (including a Green Man) and stained-glass, including fine work by the Victorian artist Kempe and the Arts and Crafts artist Christopher Whall. There are impressive tombs here too. In the Cockayne Chapel there are examples from the 15th and 16th centuries, including brasses and a magnificent example from 1447 intricately carved in alabaster. Perhaps most touching of all is the sculptor Thomas Banks's figure of Penelope Boothby, who died in 1791 aged five, lying as if asleep.

Darley Dale

Darley Dale Church. Darley Dale is a conglomeration of small villages between Matlock and Rowsley; its growth was due to the coming of the railway in the 1840s. The parish church of St Helen dates mainly from the 13th and 14th centuries, and its battlemented tower rises nobly above the valley. Inside is the tomb of John Milward, a Royalist colonel in the Civil War, whose effigy kneels with his wife and their 11 children. An older tomb is that of Sir John de Darley, who died in 1322; he is dressed in chain mail, and holds his heart in his hands.

But Darley's main claim to fame is the massive yew tree which stands in the churchyard and can be seen on the extreme right of this photograph. It has a girth of around 33ft; its age has been variously estimated at between 600 and 4,000 years, and it was almost certainly there before the church. On an outside wall of the church is a stone sundial, put up by the Rev William Wray in the 18th century; the story goes that he wanted to encourage his parishioners to be more punctual – they spent too much time gossiping under the yew.

Above left: ASHBOURNE, THE CHURCH 1886 18570

Left: DARLEY DALE, THE CHURCH 1892 31305

Opposite: BAKEWELL, ALL SAINTS' CHURCH FROM THE SOUTH-WEST 24627

Above: BAKEWELL, THE CHURCH, THE CHOIR EAST 1890 24629

Left: BAKEWELL, THE CHURCH, THE VERNON CHAPEL 1890 24632

Below left: BAKEWELL, THE CHURCH, DOROTHY VERNON'S TOMB 1890 24630

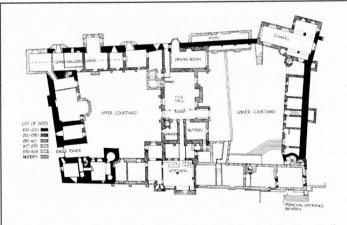

Dorothy Vernon (her tomb is pictured in 24630) lived at Haddon Hall during the 16th century and eloped with John Manners, son of the Earl of Rutland. Being the last in line, she inherited Haddon Hall, which then became part of the Rutland estate when the Manners family was ennobled.

Bakewell

All Saints' Church. The complex shape of the beautiful All Saints' Church is well shown in 24627, and the way the church spire soars above the town. The octagonal tower was built in 1841 to replace the original 14th-century spire. The Vernon Chapel in the south transept commemorates the Vernons of Haddon Hall, one of the most important families in the Peak District. At the eastern end of the chapel (24632) is the monument to Sir George Manners, who died in 1623, and his wife, Grace Pierrepoint, with their children (including a baby) praying in the arcades below their parents.

Chesterfield

The Church of St Mary and All Saints'.
Despite looking as though it is about to topple over, the spire of St Mary and All Saints' is stable. The twist is a result of the heat of the sun on the lead plates, which in turn warped the green timber underneath them. A less prosaic story is the tradition that the Devil visited Chesterfield one windy day and sat on the top of the spire so that he could have a good look at the town. To prevent himself from falling, Old Nick twisted his tail round the spire, but he was so shocked when he heard a local speak the truth that he flew off without unwinding his tail, causing the spire to twist. The earliest written record of St Mary's dates from 1100, when the church was given to the Dean and Chapter of Lincoln. The oldest part of the present structure dates from the 13th century, and both the tower and the south transept were added during the 14th century.

> During the Napoleonic Wars, Chesterfield was one of the places used to accommodate French prisoners. Allowed out during the day, the prisoners were summoned back to their quarters by the ringing of a curfew bell from St Mary's. This bell was also known as the pancake bell: it used to be rung on Shrove Tuesday to call parishioners to their annual confession.

Left: CHESTERFIELD, THE CHURCH OF ST MARY AND ALL SAINTS 1902 48888P

Adel

The Church of St John the Baptist. At first sight, Adel is an insignificant suburban village to the north of Leeds. But its great, hidden glory is its perfect little Norman church of St John the Baptist. Note the spectacular south doorway, with four orders of roll-mouldings adorned with both zigzag and beakhead decoration – it is said that the 40 beakheads on the innermost arch represent the 40 days and nights of Christ's fast in the wilderness. Above in the gable is a carving of the Paschal Lamb, symbol of John the Baptist, to whom the church is dedicated. Inside, there is more wonderful Norman carving on the capitals of the chancel arch depicting the baptism of Christ (by John the Baptist) and the Crucifixion; there are more beakheads on the arch itself. Altogether, this church is a wonderful example of Romanesque art.

Above: ADEL, THE CHURCH OF ST JOHN THE BAPTIST C1871 7413

Left: ADEL, THE CHURCH OF ST JOHN THE BAPTIST, THE SOUTH PORCH 1888 20981

Ilkley

Right: ILKLEY, THE CHURCH, SAXON
CROSSES 1911 63567

Far right: ILKLEY, THE SAXON CROSSES
IN THE CHURCHYARD C1874 7290

Ilkley Church. These three fine and justly celebrated
Saxon crosses (now kept inside All Saints' Church) are marked
with pre-Christian symbols and some later carvings. It is
believed that they were originally used as grave markers, or as
markers for the spot where the Gospel would be preached before
the church was built. The central pillar dates from AD850, and
its carvings depict the four evangelists, St Matthew, Mark, Luke
and John.

As the crosses indicate, there has been a church here since
the 7th century – the earliest church was probably built of
stone taken from the Roman fort of Olicana. The present
church dates from the Perpendicular period, but it was largely
reconstructed in about 1860; the 13th-century doorway has
been reused every time the church was rebuilt. The medieval
font, made of stone from Ilkley Moor, has a grand wooden
font cover of the 17th century. An effigy of a 14th-century
knight lies peacefully in a side chapel.

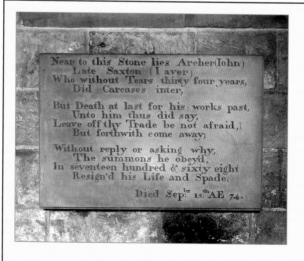

SELBY ABBEY, THE GRAVEDIGGER'S EPITAPH 1924 75676

Near to this Stone lies Archer (Iohn)
Late Saxton (I aver)
Who without Tears thirty four years,
Did Carcases inter,

But Death at last for his works past,
Unto him thus did say,
Leave off thy Trade be not afraid,
But forthwith come away;

Without reply or asking why,
The summons he obey'd,
In seventeen hundred & sixty eight
Resign'd his Life and Spade.

Died Sep:br 15:th AE 74.

Above left: YORK, GOODRAMGATE 1886 3443

Left: YORK, HOLY TRINITY CHURCH, GOODRAMGATE 1909 61857

Above right: YORK, HOLY TRINITY CHURCH, GOODRAMGATE, THE INTERIOR 1909 61858

York

Holy Trinity Church. The houses here in Goodramgate (3443), on what is called Our Lady's Row, are amongst the oldest in England, dating from the early 14th century. At the extreme left of the photograph is the brick gateway (1786, with gates of 1815) which leads to Holy Trinity Church. Once through the gateway, we are out of the bustle of the old part of the city and in a secret, secluded and quiet haven. The rather battered exterior of the church (61857) is a charming mixture of materials and styles (Decorated and Perpendicular), and the interior (61858) is even more picturesque. There does not seem to be a straight line anywhere; the attractive 17th- and 18th-century pews heave and flow like the sea around the unpretentious arcades. There is much excellent stained-glass of the 15th century, including the east window; and note the rare saddleback pitched roof.

The headless ghost of Thomas Percy, Earl of Northumberland, is said to wander here. He was captured and executed in 1572 for plotting against Elizabeth I, and ever since, or so the legend goes, he has been searching for his head.

Above: MASHAM, ST MARY'S CHURCH 1927 80262P

Masham

St Mary's stands at one corner of the vast market place. Masham market was granted trading rights from 1393, and at one time 40,000 sheep would be traded in one day. The church was wealthy, almost certainly benefiting from the sheep fairs, and was said to be the richest prebend in Yorkshire, if not the whole of England.

The church of St Mary dates from the 12th century, and outside is an even earlier carved Saxon cross. The lower part of the tower is 11th-century. But the elegant spire on its octagonal base was added during the 15th century, and it is a landmark for miles around. Inside the church is a grand Jacobean monument to Sir Marmaduke Wyvill: statues of him and his wife lie above their kneeling children.

Ribchester

Stydd Church. The Roman general Agricola established a Roman fort here in the 1st century AD, which grew into a thriving community. The tombstone of a cavalry rider and a replica of a parade helmet are what visitors come from far away to see. The original of the helmet, found by the River Ribble in 1796, is in the British Museum. In the 18th century handloom and flax weaving became important.

It is said that this venerable church, St Saviour's, is 900 years old, and that the apostle Paul preached here. It is also said that the origin of the name Stidd is 'stood', because during a severe earth tremor this was the only building undamaged.

Heysham

St Peter's Church. Heysham is a very ancient village that can easily trace its history over 2,000 years. The origins of the parish church of St Peter on Heysham Head are lost in the mists of time. The earliest recorded date is 1080, when it was noted as an old Saxon church (this original part is at the centre of the building). There was probably an even earlier church on this site built by the Angles. Some of the Saxon stonework remains today, even though the church has been added to and enlarged. The old oak screen between nave and chancel is believed to have come from Cockersands Abbey.

> The hogback stone (64232), which marked the grave of a Viking warrior, marked his resting spot for over 1,000 years: it is from the 10th century. He had converted to Christianity, but though one side of the stone is carved with Christian symbols, the other side represents the pagan Viking heaven. In 1961 the stone was taken inside the church for protection against the weather and to save it from too many visitors running their hands over it.

Top left: RIBCHESTER, STYDD CHURCH 1894 34328

Above right: HEYSHAM, ST PETER'S CHURCH 1888 21072

Right: HEYSHAM, ST PETER'S CHURCH, THE HOGBACK STONE 1912 64232

Gisburn

Above: GISBURN, THE CHURCH 1921 71201

A racehorse helped to pay for the new organ installed in St Mary's in 1862. This was Flambeau, owned by Lord Ribblesdale, who raced him in France. Lord Ribblesdale raffled Flambeau at a bazaar to raise funds for the splendid new instrument.

Gisburn Church. Guy of Gisburn, of Robin Hood fame, was said to have come from this village. In 1260 a charter was granted to Sawley Abbey to hold a fair in Gisburn. The local lords were the Lister family, many of whom lie in the church, and the Ribblesdales, whose tombs are in the Ribblesdale Chapel. The ancient church stands in the centre of the village. It is dedicated to St Mary the Virgin, though it is thought that at one time it had a dual dedication to St Mary the Virgin and St Andrew. This could have been because the north of England was much troubled by raids from the Scots, and to have a church dedicated to the patron saint of Scotland would have saved it from attack. Also, the patrons of the living were at one time the prioress and nuns of Stainfield Nunnery in Lincolnshire, which was dedicated to St Mary the Virgin and St Andrew.

Gisburn appears in the Domesday Book, and early records show that there was probably a church here in about 1135. Certainly, part of the arcade dates from the 12th century, but this may have been brought from Sawley Abbey after the Dissolution. The south door is 13th-century, enclosed by a 15th-century porch. The battlemented upper part of the tower is 14th-century. Oliver Cromwell stabled horses and billeted troops in the church after the Battle of Preston in 1648. The churchyard of St Mary's is glorious with snowdrops in winter. An unusual headstone is that of Jenny Preston, showing a witch with her cauldron.

Kirk Braddan

The Isle of Man was settled by the Vikings in the 9th century. As the Vikings became Christian they adopted and adapted the Celtic crosses, and often added pagan images to them. The tall slender Kirk Braddan Cross is a beautiful example of Viking art in the Mammen style (named from a place in Denmark). It has interlaced dragons on its faces and a runic inscription on the edge.

Kirk Braddan Church. This church is 'the old church' because a new church was built nearby in 1876; the old church was too small for the growing congregations caused by the tourism industry, and for a while services were held in the old churchyard and a field before the new church was built. This old former parish church, built on an ancient site, was rebuilt in 1777. Since it escaped Victorian restoration, it contains its original box pews, gallery, and three-decker pulpit (with its lectern, minister's pew, and pulpit above). Inside the church today are several Celtic and Norse crosses dating from about AD800 to 1250, including the ones we can see in photograph 33020. Despite the comparative modernity of both churches, the site has an ancient past, as the crosses reveal. The church is dedicated to St Brendan (or Braddan), a Celtic saint, and it is thought that the first church here was built in about AD400.

Left: KIRK BRADDAN, RUNIC CROSSES 1893 33020

Below left: KIRK BRADDAN, THE OLD CHURCH 1907 59172

Below right: KIRK BRADDAN, THE OLD CHURCH 1893 33018

Cartmel

The Priory Church. Cartmel has been described as a cathedral city in miniature. The magnificent late 12th-century priory church of St Mary and St Michael was founded by William Marshall, Baron of Cartmel and later 1st Earl of Pembroke, and was never promoted to the status of an abbey. Much of the early documentation of the priory has been lost, including the precise date of its founding some time between 1189 and 1219. Because the priory church was used by the parish, it survived the Dissolution of the Monasteries in the 1530s, when it was ordered 'that it stand still'.

In photograph 34098 we can see the striking cross-set belfry rising above a low square tower – the belfry was added in the 15th century, and inside the church the massive supporting piers can be seen. The choir stall seats and benches are believed to date from around 1430 to 1440, while the screens and canopies are later. Of the misericords, only one has been lost (64383 shows one of them, a carving of a Green Man). A number of them are the heads of real or imaginary beasts, and most have foliage.

Top: CARTMEL, THE PRIORY CHURCH, SOUTH SIDE 1894 34098

Far left: CARTMEL, THE PRIORY CHURCH, ANCIENT CHAIRS 1894 64378

Left: CARTMEL, THE PRIORY CHURCH, THE CHOIR STALLS 1912 64380

Bottom: CARTMEL, THE PRIORY CHURCH, A MISERICORD 1912 64383

Kendal

Above: KENDAL, HOLY TRINITY PARISH CHURCH 1896 38532

Above: KENDAL, HOLY TRINITY CHURCH, THE VIEW ACROSS THE CHOIR 1924 75811

Right: KENDAL, HOLY TRINITY CHURCH, THE FONT 1924 75812

Holy Trinity Church. A church in Kendal is recorded in Domesday Book. No trace of this Saxon church exists, but a fragment of an Anglian cross in the present church may have come from this earlier one. Kendal's parish church is dedicated to the Holy and Undivided Trinity. It is one of the widest parish churches in England, with five aisles. Its size is an indication of the wealth of the medieval town - this wealth was derived from one commodity, wool. Building began in the 13th century, and the south aisle, known as the Flemish Aisle, was added in the 14th century. It was said to have been built and so called because Flemish weavers came as refugees to the town at this time.

High up on the north wall hangs a helmet and sword, said to date from the time of the Civil War. The story is that the helmet belonged to a Royalist, Sir Robert Phillipson, sometimes known as Robin the Devil. He is said to have lost his helmet when he rode into the church on horseback, looking for his Parliamentarian enemy Colonel Briggs, who had besieged Phillipson's house. However, no-one seems to know who owned the sword.

The proximity of the River Kent meant that the church was prone to flooding. One especially bad flood in 1671 is said to have left 'much ffish' in the churchyard. The threat of flooding in Kendal remained until the 1970s, when extensive flood protection work was undertaken.

The 15th-century black marble font (75812) has an intricately-carved font cover by John Mark Kirkbride of Sedbergh; it was presented in 1898 by 'the ladies of the parish'. The memorial on a pillar near the font (75812, left foreground) is to George Romney, the portrait painter. The inscription reads: 'So long as Genius and Talent shall be respected his Fame will live.' Romney lived for a time in Kendal, and was married in Holy Trinity in 1756. He spent most of his working life in London, but eventually returned to Kendal and died here in 1802. He is buried in his birthplace, Dalton-in-Furness.

Grasmere

Above: GRASMERE, THE CHURCH OF ST OSWALD 1926 79209

Above right top: GRASMERE, THE CHURCH OF ST OSWALD
AND THE RECTORY 1929 82835

Above right bottom: GRASMERE, THE CHURCH OF ST OSWALD,
THE INTERIOR 1912 64336

Left: GRASMERE, THE CHURCH OF ST OSWALD,
THE MEMORIAL TO WORDSWORTH 1929 82839x

The Church of St Oswald.
Grasmere's church is perhaps best known for being the last resting place of the poet William Wordsworth, who is buried here alongside his wife, Mary, and his sister and constant companion, Dorothy. He planted eight yew trees in the churchyard, one marking his and Mary's grave, and in 82839x we see his memorial in the church. Wordsworth and his sister Dorothy lived at Dove Cottage, which he rented for £8 a year, from 1799 to 1813. He called Grasmere 'the loveliest spot that man hath ever found'. Close by is the tranquil lake from which the village gets its name.

A contemporary guidebook describes Grasmere's parish church of St Oswald as 'a massive but barnlike structure, which no one with an eye to the picturesque would wish to see altered'. It is one of Lakeland's oldest churches, and is named after a 7th-century Christian king of Northumberland, who is believed to have preached on this site. The church has a sturdy, rough-hewn look, and as we can see from 64336, it is notable for a two-storey arcade (dating from the 17th century) and a tangle of black beams. Wordsworth vividly described St Oswald's roof as being upheld
'By naked rafters intricately crossed,
Like leafless underboughs, mid some thick grove,
All withered by the depth of shade above'.

Rushbearing

Originally church floors were made of beaten earth and covered in rushes, and it was commonplace to bury people inside the church as well as in the churchyard. On the church's saint's day, parishioners would bring fresh rushes and herbs to strew on the church floor to purify the air and help keep the worshippers' feet warm and dry. This festivity was known as rushbearing, and continued until as recently as the 1800s – after that, the floors were flagged or tiled. However, the ancient custom is still alive in some Cumbrian parishes, where rushes and flowers are paraded round the village in procession: a band is followed by the clergy and then by the children, who carry a rush or flower cross, which is brought to the church.

Penrith

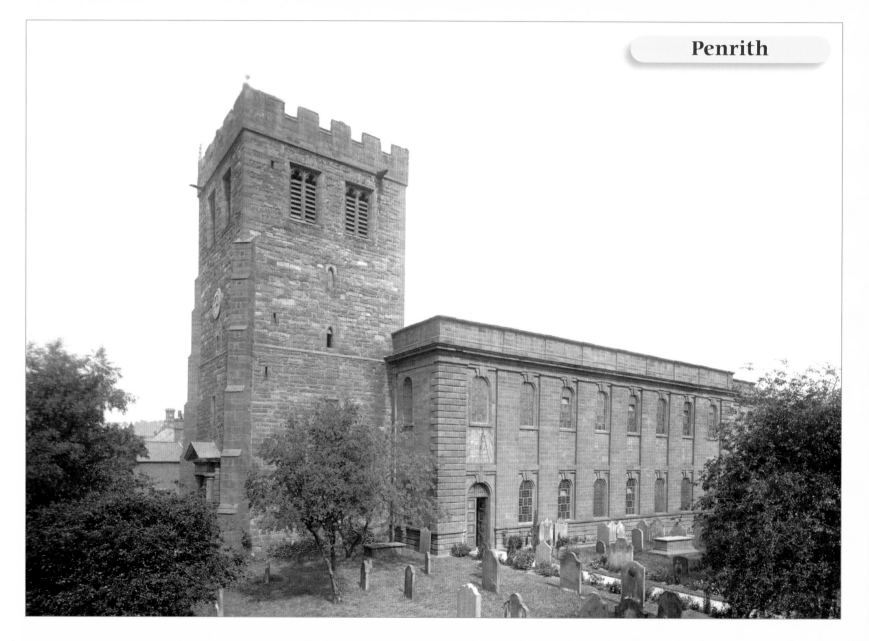

Above: PENRITH, ST ANDREW'S CHURCH 1893 32924

St Andrew's Church. The massive tower of St Andrew's Church is mainly Norman work, built of red sandstone with walls 6ft thick. When it was built, Penrith was troubled by border warfare, and the tower was used as a shelter and strongpoint. The rest of the church was rebuilt in the 1720s in the classical style to a design by Hawksmoor. Inside are murals painted by a local artist, Jacob Thompson.

The Giant's Grave in St Andrew's churchyard is actually a collection of two badly weathered 10th-century cross shafts and four Norse 'hogback' tombstones. Stories about the grave have been linked not only with the mythical giant Sir Owen Caesarius and the Arthurian legends, but also with Owain, son of Urien, a 6th-century King of Rheged, and Owen, King of Cumbria from AD920 to AD937. The Giant's Thumb stands close to the Giant's Grave and is another badly eroded stone cross dating to about the year AD920. In later years, the Giant's Thumb was used as a public pillory.

Above left: PENRITH, THE GIANT'S GRAVE 1893 32926

Above right: PENRITH, THE GIANT'S THUMB 1893 32927

The carvings on both the Giant's Thumb and the Giant's Grave show an intriguing mixture of Anglian, Celtic and Norse decorative motifs, indicating that in the 10th century the area around Penrith must have been something of a cultural melting pot.

Upleatham

Upleatham Church. One of Cleveland's famous landmarks, the Old Church at Upleatham (near Guisborough and Middlesbrough) stands on the site of an earlier Saxon church. Dating from Norman times, and incorporating 17th-century work, it was abandoned as a place of worship in 1836, and much of it was subsequently demolished. This led to the claim in later years that it was 'the smallest church in England' at 17ft 9 inches by 13ft. It lies in an isolated site outside the village, and is dedicated to St Andrew. It is now a redundant church, but in 2002 a Benedictine monk said Mass here, the first held at the church for 500 years.

Above: UPLEATHAM, THE CHURCH C1960 U16002

Left: UPLEATHAM, THE CHURCH C1885 18139

Above: ESCOMB, THE SAXON CHURCH 1898 41463

Escomb

The Saxon Church. The small 7th-century church of St John the Evangelist is one of the finest examples of early Christian architecture in the north. Built largely from stone salvaged from the abandoned Roman fort at Binchester, St John's lay semi-derelict in the 1870s; it might well have been allowed to fall into complete ruin, had it not been for the Reverend R E Hooppell, who recognised St John's importance and launched an appeal to save it. Now, tiny, dark, and plain, it looks much as it did in Saxon times. The long nave and narrow chancel are typical of Northumbrian ecclesiastical architecture of the period. The churchyard is circular, as a Celtic church's would be. Later additions include a 12th-century porch and 13th- and 19th-century windows.

In the late 18th century, Wallsend's local church of Holy Cross at Willington Gut was roofless and unusable. The schoolroom was pressed into service as a replacement church, and all went well for about 10 years. Then in 1806 the Dean and Chapter caused chaos and alarm by announcing that as the schoolroom had never been consecrated, all weddings that had taken place there were invalid. Even worse, all the couples that had 'married' there were technically living in sin, and all children born to them were illegitimate. The result was the building of St Peter's, in some haste, on the hill above the local ropeworks.

St Paul's Church. The chancel of the Saxon church of St Paul dates from the 7th century; it was once the church of the Venerable Bede's monastery. Inside the church is a stone slab inscribed with an inscription recording the dedication of the church on 23 April AD685. The tower was built in the late 11th century. Close by are the remains of the Benedictine monastery which was built on the site of the important Anglo-Saxon monastery where the Venerable Bede lived and worked (AD673-735). Bede is renowned for being the first English historian, and his work 'The Ecclesiastical History of the English Nation' is valuable source material for historians of this period. Bede was also responsible for devising the AD and BC dating system for dates before and after the birth of Christ.

Recorded on the grave of a
Newcastle architect at Gateshead:

ROBERT TROLLOPE
Here lies Robert Trollope
Who made these stones roll up;
When death took his soul up,
His body filled this hole up.

Bede's chair, in St Paul's Church, Jarrow, is thought to have belonged to the Venerable Bede (AD673-735), the chronicler monk who spent most of his life in the monastery at Jarrow. For centuries, this ancient oak chair was popularly believed to influence marriage and childbirth. Unmarried girls placed splinters from the chair beneath their pillows so that they would dream of their future husbands. Brides sat in it after the wedding ceremony to ensure fertility, while mothers-to-be soaked wood chips carved from the chair in water and then drank the liquid in the hope that it would ease the pangs of childbirth.

Jarrow

Recorded on a tombstone in a
Newcastle upon Tyne cemetery:

Here lies a man, who all his mortal life,
Spent mending clocks, but could not mend his wife.
The alarm of his bell was never so shrill,
As was her tongue clacking like a mill.
But now he's gone – of whither none can tell –
I hope beyond the sound of his wife's yell.

St Mary's contains the only medieval wooden sculpture of its kind in Britain. This is a huge reclining oak figure of the patriarch Jesse, who holds the branch of a tree growing from his body. This was the base of a sculpture showing the family tree of Jesus, who was descended from Jesse, the father of King David; this sculpture may have formed the reredos of the old high altar.

Abergavenny

St Mary's Church. Abergavenny lies in a wonderful setting in the valley of the Usk, overlooked by majestic mountains – the Sugar Loaf, the Blorenge and the two Skirrids (Ysgyryd Fawr and Ysgyryd Fach). After the Dissolution of the Monasteries in 1542, the church of Abergavenny Priory became St Mary's Parish Church. The nave was almost completely rebuilt during restorations in 1882 and 1896, but the choir and sanctuary, the oldest parts of the church, date from the 12th to the 14th century, and are crowned by an 18th-century vaulted roof. The east window has colourful stained-glass, a memorial to Brigadier Barker who was killed in action in the First World War.

In the 15th and 16th centuries the Herbert family prospered in their family home at Raglan Castle. Sir William Herbert, for instance, was thought to be the most powerful man in Wales from 1465 until his death in 1469. He was not buried at St Mary's but at Tintern Abbey. Other members of his family are buried in the Herbert Chapel (32601s) in three magnificent alabaster tombs. In the centre is his father William ap Thomas, who took the name Herbert, and his wife Gwladys. In the foreground are William's brother Sir Richard Herbert of Coldbrook and his wife Margaret. To the left is the elaborate arched tomb of William's natural son Sir Richard Herbert of Ewyas.

Above left: ABERGAVENNY, ST MARY'S CHURCH 1898 41681s

Left: ABERGAVENNY, THE CHURCH, THE INTERIOR OF THE HERBERT CHAPEL 1893 32601s

Above: LLANDOUGH, ST DOCHDWY'S CHURCH
C1955 L280012

Llandough

In 1803 minerals were found on the Earl of Bute's estate at Llandough: there were alabaster, fuller's earth and black marble workings here.

St Dochdwy's Church. St Dochdwy's stands on top of Llandough Hill, and its unusual saddleback-roofed bell tower can be seen from as far away as Caerphilly Mountain. Built on the site of a monastery founded by St Dochdwy or Dochau, the name by which St Cyngar was better known, the present church dates from the 1860s, although it incorporates the original Norman chancel arch (now linking the south aisle to the bell tower). The new church was designed by S C Fripp in a neo-Gothic style similar to Butterfield's using polychromatic brickwork (William Butterfield, a far more eminent architect, was working on a nearby church at the time). In the churchyard is the Irbic Cross, dating from the 9th century. This reminds us that Llandough has been a holy place since the 5th century, when St Dochdwy set up his Christian community here. Although much eroded by weather, the cross is adorned by an interlaced rope pattern and various sculptures, including a horse and its rider.

Who was St Cenydd? Legend says that he was born in the 6th century with a withered leg, and was therefore cast adrift in a basket on the Loughor estuary. He was rescued by seagulls, and cared for by angels.

Rhosili

St Mary's Church. Rhosili village overlooks the often windswept Rhosili Bay on the western edge of the Gower Peninsula. It is enclosed by an ancient open-field system, the Viel: strips of land known as landshares are bounded by low stone walls, a remarkable survival of medieval farming methods. Tradition has it that the village is named after St Fili, who was possibly a son of St Cenydd. St Mary's is a typically simple and sturdy Gower church with a saddleback tower and a fine Norman doorway. Inside the church we can see a memorial to Petty Officer Edgar Evans, born in the village, who died with Scott in his fateful Antarctic expedition in 1912.

Llangennith

St Cenydd's Church. This church is the largest church on the Gower. It was originally founded as a priory in the 6th century by St Cenydd; a slab carved with intricate Celtic knotwork designs now inside the church is said to be his gravestone, but it is actually part of a 9th-century Celtic cross. The priory was ransacked by Viking raiders in the 10th century. The present church was rebuilt around 1140 by Caradoc of Rhos, and Henry de Beaumont, Norman lord of Gower, handed the priory over to the Benedictine monks from St Taurin in France. The huge saddle-backed tower is in an unusual position, north of the nave. The 13th-century carved effigy of a knight from the de la Mare family lies in the church – he is nicknamed 'Dolly Mare'.

A ghostly coach is said to drive along Rhosili sands on wild nights. It belonged to a member of the Lucas family, who made a fortune thanks to the 'dollar ship'. This ship was wrecked here in the 17th century bringing the dowry of Catherine of Braganza (wife of Charles II) to Britain, and many silver coins were found in the early 19th century, causing a 'silver rush'.

Top left: RHOSILI, ST MARY'S CHURCH 1901 47970

Above left: LLANGENNITH, ST CENYDD'S CHURCH 1937 87973

Pembrey

Above: PEMBREY, ST ILLTYD'S CHURCH 1936 87819

St Illtyd's Church. The tall tower of St Illtyd's Church is Norman, and the timber roof is 16th-century. In the churchyard is a monument to a French soldier, Colonel Coquilin, and his daughter Adeline. They were drowned when their ship, the 'Jeanne Emma', struck the Cefn Sidan sands. The inscription states that Adeline was 'the niece of Josephine, consort to the renowned individual Napoleon Bonaparte'.

According to S Lewis's 'Topographical Dictionary of Wales' (1833), Pembrey's name comes from 'pen bre', 'head of a hill or promontory'; Pembrey's situation is 'at the extremity of a mountainous ridge, beyond which a low promontory extends into the bay of Carmarthen … The substrata abound with mineral wealth, this district being thought to be the richest in South Wales in both bituminous and hard coal, both being worked to a very great extent. The quality of the soft coal is peculiarly adapted to the production of gas, the working of iron, and other manufacturing purposes'.

St Govan's Head

St Govan's Head Chapel. The present chapel is 13th-century and contains an altar, a bench and a cell hewn out of the rock. It is thought that the original chapel or hermitage dates from the 5th century. Legends about its origins abound. One has it that it was the retreat of Cofen, wife of a king of Glamorgan; another that this is where Sir Gawaine became a hermit after King Arthur's death. A third is as follows: 'Here, according to a curious old legend, St Govan sought shelter from his pagan enemies; whereupon the massy rock closed over him and hid him from his pursuers, opening again to release the pious anchorite as soon as the chase was overpassed' (H Thornhill Timmins, 1895). It is said that the steps leading from the cliff top never count the same going up as going down. It is a wonderful experience to stand 'on the bold jutting promontory of St Govan, looking out upon that broad ocean, whose ever-rolling waves fitly suggest the idea of eternity' (Thomas Roscoe, 1820).

> Yet another legend about St Govan's Chapel says that the chapel's silver bell was once stolen by pirates whose ship was promptly wrecked, killing all on board. The bell was recovered and encased in rock, which would ring out when struck.

Gwbert-on-Sea

Mwnt Church. The Teifi begins its journey to the sea 70 miles away - it provided an inland route for the Normans to service the castles of Cardigan and Cilgerran. However, the river becomes very shallow at the broad and sandy estuary, restricting boat movements to a brief period at high tide, but providing a good place to fish with nets. At Mwnt, with its beautiful beach and its mountain rising behind, stands this isolated church. It was probably established during the 6th century, but not built in stone until after 1300. It is one of only a few churches in the county untouched by the Victorian restorers, and still retains its bellcote and whitewash.

This was a pilgrims' church, used by devout souls on the taxing pilgrims' route from Bardsey Island at the top of the Lleyn peninsula round Cardigan Bay to St Davids in the far south-west. To make the hard journey along this rugged coast to the shrine of St David ensured each pilgrim a place in heaven. This simple chapel must have offered welcome respite to weary travellers.

Top: ST GOVAN'S HEAD, THE CHAPEL 1890 24928

Above: GWBERT-ON-SEA, MWNT CHURCH C1965 G172111

Clynnogfawr

Above: CLYNNOGFAWR, ST BEUNO'S CHURCH
C1955 C561054

St Beuno's possesses a pair of wooden tongs, once a common sight in old country churches. These were used against dogs; not to remove them during the services, but simply to prevent them from fighting!

St Beuno's Church. The relatively large, early 16th-century church of St Beuno dominates the small village of Clynnogfawr. The church, which has a wonderfully plain interior but a fine roof and rood screen and misericords in the chancel, was a stopping place for pilgrims on their way to, or from, Ynys Enlii (Bardsey Island), an important place of pilgrimage in Britain during the Middle Ages. It was said that two pilgrimages to Bardsey were the equivalent of going to Rome.

The church stands on the site of a much earlier one, built in the 7th century; it is dedicated to St Beuno, who is said to have come here to Clynnogfawr in about AD635, and to have founded many churches hereabouts. He was buried in his own cell, now a chapel on the south side of the church. Near the church is St Beuno's Well – its water was said to cure all ills. In the church is the Chest of Beuno, an ancient oak strong-box, said to be so sturdy that it is impossible to break it.

Conwy

Above: CONWY, ST MARY'S CHURCH, THE CHURCHYARD AND THE GRAVE THAT INSPIRED WORDSWORTH'S 'WE ARE SEVEN' 1913 65764

St Mary's Church. Conwy has always been a gateway to Caernarvonshire and Anglesey. Edward I built his great castle here after the conquest of Gwynedd in 1282 to control this strategic river crossing. In the 19th century both Thomas Telford's suspension bridge and Robert Stephenson's tubular railway bridge were located here. The church was part of the Cistercian abbey founded in 1184, of which little remains. Much of the present church is 13th-century, and there was a programme of restoration in the 19th century. Inside is a 15th-century carved screen and a Tudor font. The photograph opposite shows the remnants of an old gravestone, said to cover the grave which inspired Wordsworth's poem 'We are Seven'.

WE ARE SEVEN

… A simple child,
That lightly draws its breath,
And feels its life in every limb,
What should it know of death?

I met a little cottage girl:
She was eight years old, she said;
Her hair was thick with many a curl
That clustered round her head.

She had a rustic, woodland air,
And she was wildly clad:
Her eyes were fair, and very fair;
- Her beauty made me glad.

'Sisters and brothers, little Maid,
How many may you be?'
'How many? Seven in all,' she said
And wondering looked at me.

'And where are they? I pray you tell.'
She answered, 'Seven are we;
And two of us at Conway dwell,
And two are gone to sea.

Two of us in the church-yard lie,
My sister and my brother;
And, in the church-yard cottage, I
Dwell near them with my mother.'

'You say that two at Conway dwell,
And two are gone to sea,
Yet ye are seven! - I pray you tell,
Sweet Maid, how this may be.'

Then did the little Maid reply,
'Seven boys and girls are we;
Two of us in the church-yard lie,
Beneath the church-yard tree.'

'You run about, my little Maid,
Your limbs they are alive;
If two are in the church-yard laid,
Then ye are only five.'

'Their graves are green, they may be seen,'
The little Maid replied,
'Twelve steps or more from my mother's door,
And they are side by side.

My stockings there I often knit,
My kerchief there I hem;
And there upon the ground I sit,
And sing a song to them.

And often after sunset, Sir,
When it is light and fair,
I take my little porringer,
And eat my supper there.

The first that died was sister Jane;
In bed she moaning lay,
Till God released her of her pain;
And then she went away.

So in the church-yard she was laid;
And, when the grass was dry,
Together round her grave we played,
My brother John and I.

'And when the ground was white with snow,
And I could run and slide,
My brother John was forced to go,
And he lies by her side.'

'How many are you, then,' said I,
'If they two are in heaven?'
Quick was the little Maid's reply,
'O Master! we are seven.'

'But they are dead; those two are dead!
Their spirits are in heaven!'
'Twas throwing words away; for still
The little Maid would have her will,
And said, 'Nay, we are seven!'

WILLIAM WORDSWORTH (1770-1850)

Above: BODFARI, THE DINORBEN ARMS AND THE CHURCH C1960 B461040P

Bodfari

Bodfari Church. This area near St Asaph has a long history – there is an Iron Age hill-fort nearby – but Bodfari itself was a tiny place until comparatively recently, with about four houses in the 18th century and only a few more by 1845. It is said that the Church of St Stephen dates from the 7th century; Bodfari may be the 'Boteuuarul' of the Domesday Book and the 'Batavari' mentioned in 1093, but the church is certainly recorded in a taxation record of 1254 as the church at 'Bottewara'. In medieval times there was a holy well here named after St Deifer, once the patron saint of the church. St Stephen's was much altered in 1865, and now the earliest part surviving is the late medieval tower.

THOMAS CARLYLE

Ecclefechan

Hoddam Church. Hoddam is situated in south Dumfriesshire near the River Annan and bordering Ecclefechan, the birthplace of the historian and essayist Thomas Carlyle (1795-1881). The author of 'The French Revolution', 'Past and Present', and 'Frederick the Great' lived for much of his life in London, but was buried in his birthplace (E120008).

'Hoddam parish generally is richly embellished with hedgerows, clumps of wood, and high cultivation, and combines, with surrounding heights, to form a finely picturesque landscape', says Groome's 'Ordnance Gazetteer of Scotland'(1882-84). Skene's 'Celtic Scotland' (1877) tells us that when in AD573 St Kentigern returned from Wales to southern Scotland, 'King Rydderch Hael and his people went forth to meet him, and they encountered each other at a place called Holdelm, now Hoddam … Here he fixed his see for a time; but afterwards, warned by divine revelation, he transferred it to his own city Glasgow'. The parish church was built in 1817 in early Gothic Revival style.

Top: ECCLEFECHAN, HODDAM CHURCH C1955 E120010

Above: ECCLEFECHAN, THE GRAVE OF THOMAS CARLYLE C1955 E120008

Alloway

Above: ALLOWAY, THE KIRK 1897 39861

Above right: ALLOWAY, PORTRAIT OF ROBERT BURNS 1897 39858A

Alloway Church. Scotland's most celebrated poet Robert Burns was born in Alloway on 25 January 1759. Burns's verses are famous the world over. He died at the early age of 37 in Dumfries. In 1881 his cottage was purchased by the trustees of the Burns Monument and opened as a museum. The pleasant village of Alloway is now the centre of pilgrimage for lovers of Burns's poetry.

Robert Burns played in this churchyard as a boy, and the popular legends about hauntings and the ghostly atmosphere of the roofless ruin affected him deeply. He used the kirk and the Auld Brig o'Doon near by as scenes for his celebrated ghost story 'Tam o' Shanter', which first appeared in The Edinburgh Review in 1791 (right). Burns's father, who had repaired the kirk wall to keep the sheep at bay, is buried in the churchyard.

'THIS church stands by the river, a small distance from the bridge of Doon, on the road leading from Maybole to Ayr. About a century ago it was united to the parish of Ayr; since which time it has fallen to ruins. It is one of the eldest parishes in Scotland, and still retains these privileges: the minister of Ayr is obliged to marry and baptize in it, and also here to hold his parochial catechisings … This church is also famous for being the place wherein the witches and warlocks used to hold their infernal meetings, or sabbaths, and prepare their magical unctions; here too they used to amuse themselves with dancing to the pipes of the muckle-horned Deel. Diverse stories of these horrid rites are still current; one of which my worthy friend Mr Burns has here favoured me with in verse.'

FRANCIS GROSE, 'THE ANTIQUITIES OF SCOTLAND', 1797

> WHEN chapman billies leave the street,
> And drouthy neibors, neibors, meet;
> As market days are wearing late,
> And folk begin to tak the gate,
> While we sit bousing at the nappy,
> An' getting fou and unco happy,
> We think na on the lang Scots miles,
> The mosses, waters, slaps and stiles,
> That lie between us and our hame,
> Where sits our sulky, sullen dame,
> Gathering her brows like gathering storm,
> Nursing her wrath to keep it warm.
> This truth fand honest Tam o' Shanter,
> As he frae Ayr ae night did canter:
> (Auld Ayr, wham ne'er a town surpasses,
> For honest men and bonie lasses).
> O Tam! had'st thou but been sae wise,
> As taen thy ain wife Kate's advice!
> She tauld thee weel thou was a skellum,
> A blethering, blustering, drunken blellum …
> That at the Lord's house, ev'n on Sunday,
> Thou drank wi' Kirkton Jean till Monday,
> She prophesied that late or soon,
> Thou wad be found, deep drown'd in Doon,
> Or catch'd wi' warlocks in the mirk,
> By Alloway's auld, haunted kirk.

ROBERT BURNS, FROM 'TAM O'SHANTER'

Gourock

Old Gourock and Ashton Parish Church.
Gourock lies on the south shore of the Firth of Clyde some three miles west of Greenock. It wraps around Kempock Point, which projects into the Firth between Gourock Bay and West Bay. Both sides of the town climb towards the summit of Tower Hill, which commands extensive views over the Firth of Clyde to the mountains beyond.

The tower that gives Tower Hill its name was erected as a viewpoint by the local laird in 1847. East of Tower Hill is the old focus of Gourock, the Gourock Burn. Alongside the burn the Earls of Douglas built Gourock Castle, of which nothing now remains. It was demolished in 1747 and used as a quarry to build the nearby Gourock House: itself since demolished.

Gourock's story has always been closely tied to the story of the Firth of Clyde. In the early 1600s it existed as a linear village on the road running along the coast west from Greenock to Cloch Point, which was the embarkation point for the ferry to Dunoon.

Today, Cloch Point is home to a lighthouse first lit in 1797 and lies just beyond the western end of Gourock as it spreads around the mouth of the inner Firth of Clyde.

Above: GOUROCK, OLD GOUROCK AND ASHTON PARISH CHURCH, ROYAL STREET 1900 45982

Right: IRVINE, THE PARISH CHURCH 1904 53158

Since medieval times, there have been seven main trade guilds in Irvine: Hammermen, Weavers, Tailors, Cordiners, Skinners, Wrights and Squaremen, and Coopers. In 1646 they decided to unite and gain official recognition as Irvine Incorporated Trades under a Seal of Cause. Irvine town council agreed to this, on condition that the trades would not act 'in a mutinous and hostile way against them (the council) on pain of losing all their privileges'. Irvine Incorporated Trades still exist, and also perform charitable work.

Irvine

The Parish Church. Irvine, named after the River Irvine, was created a Royal Burgh in 1372 by Robert II, and its harbour has long been an important one. In the 18th century, Irvine was the largest town in Ayrshire. It was at this time that the decision was made to build the present parish church – 'the Big Kirk' – for the old church was far too small for the growing population. Building began in 1770, and the striking tower and spire were completed in 1774. The large, light, plain design is a typical post-Reformation building, although today the church is embellished by many stained-glass windows. However, the history of the church goes much farther back. The first church here was founded in the early 9th century by a Celtic saint, St Inan. Much later, in the 12th century, a new church dedicated to St Mary was erected; it was a small stone cruciform building, and wood panelling from this church can be seen in Irvine Burns Club. It was this tiny church that was succeeded by the present church.

Left: LINLITHGOW, ST MICHAEL'S CHURCH AND LINLITHGOW PALACE 1897 39158

St Michael's has been used for other purposes besides worship over the years. In 1301 Edward I of England used it as a garrison storehouse. Much later, in 1620, part of the church was a wood store; then in 1645 it briefly became Edinburgh University – the students and professors escaped here from the plague raging in the city. In 1646, Cromwellian troops were billeted in St Michael's, and their horses were stabled in the nave.

Linlithgow

The early 19th century was the era of bodysnatchers. In 1819 the Linlithgow Mortsafe Society was formed. The society hired out a metal cage to enclose a recent grave so that grave robbers could not steal the body and sell it to the medical schools in Edinburgh, and three watchmen were employed to look out for any 'resurrection men'.

St Michael's Church. Situated approximately halfway between Stirling and Edinburgh, Linlithgow was for centuries an important and favourite royal residence. Mary Queen of Scots was born in Linlithgow Palace in 1542, and baptised in the church. St Michael is the patron saint of town and church, and 'St Michael is kinde to strangers' is the motto of Linlithgow. In photograph 39158, there is a medieval carving of St Michael on top of the buttress to the far left.

The first record of St Michael's is in 1138, though there may well have been a church here before then. In 1424 there was a disastrous fire, and over the next 100 years or so the church was largely rebuilt, resulting in the building we see today. Money for this was raised by taxing ale and leather - and fining those who overpriced market goods! Outside, the church was adorned with carvings of saints and a stone 'crown' on the tower; inside, there were eight altars, windows with ornate tracery, and a glorious oak ceiling. By the late 18th century the church was in a parlous state; then in 1812 a disastrous 'restoration' was made – the oak roof was done away with – and in 1820 the stone crown was so dangerous that it had to go too. However, between 1894 and 1896 a major reinstatement of the church's former glories took place.

Muthill

Above: MUTHILL, THE OLD CHURCH 1899   44383

The Old Church. This is a very ancient religious site, for a group of Culdee monks set up a community here in the 8th century (the name Culdee derives from a Latinised form of Old Irish, and means 'companion of God'). The tower dates from the 11th century, and would originally have stood separate from its accompanying church; it might well have been used as a refuge in times of unrest or war. The ivy-covered arches clinging to the tower are the ruins of a 15th-century church. From the picturesque churchyard, where unusual metal grave markers mingle with the traditional tombstones, it is possible to see the Presbyterian church of 1826 and the Episcopalian church of 1836. Some of the Episcopalians wanted to build their new church on the site of the old one, but residents did not want the graves to be built over.

Loch Achray

Above: LOCH ACHRAY, THE TROSSACHS CHURCH 1871 L89001P

The Trossachs Church. Loch Achray is a small loch sandwiched between Loch Katrine and Loch Vennachar. The loch, which is ringed by hills, features in Sir Walter Scott's poem 'The Lady of the Lake'. Loch Katrine is said to get its name from the Highland caterans, or brigands, who lived here in the hidden glens and drove their stolen cattle through the Bealach-nam-Bo ('pass of the cattle') near the eastern end of Loch Katrine. The Trossachs ('rough country') is the name for the narrow wooded gorge between Loch Katrine and Loch Affray. The tiny Trossachs Church stands in what must be one of the most peaceful and scenic areas of the country; it is hardly surprising that this idyllic spot is a favourite venue for weddings.

The Trossachs were the scene for a famously disastrous holiday. In the 1850s, the writer and critic John Ruskin and his wife Effie came here with the young painter John Everett Millais, and it poured with rain most of the time. But the main catastrophe was that Effie and Millais fell in love. Effie was later to obtain an annulment of her marriage to Ruskin, and she and Millais married. However, the holiday did produce a masterpiece: the magnificent portrait of Ruskin standing on a rock looking at a highland stream painted by Millais.

The Rev Dr James Robertson, minister at St Kessog's, Ancaster Square in the 1790s, wrote one of Scotland's first tourist guides: 'A Pamphlet Descriptive of the Neighbourhood of Callander'. This brought the beauties of the Trossachs to the notice of the general public, a popularisation process that would be continued by Sir Walter Scott (1771-1832) in his novels and poems.

Above: CALLANDER, THE CHURCH AND THE TOWN FROM THE RIVER
1899 44629

In Elgin Cathedral

Here lie I, Martin Elginbrodde:
Ha'e mercy o' my soul, Lord God,
As I wad do, were I Lord God
And ye were Martin Elginbrodde.

Callander

Callander Church. Callander is situated in the heart of the Trossachs where the Rivers Teith and Leny meet, near three lochs – Loch Vennachar, Loch Achray and Loch Lubnaig. The history of the church here is a long one. St Kessog, a disciple of St Columba, was based at Loch Lomond, and came here evangelising in the 6th century. He is said to have preached from a hillock in Callander Meadows, now known as Tom-na-Kessaig (the hill of Kessog), and nearby Callander's first church was built. Little changed in the Highlands until the final defeat of the Jacobites at Culloden in 1746. The Highland Clearances meant that a displaced population had to be housed in the towns, and in Callander new houses were built in Ancaster Square, along with a new parish church (the church with a spire to the left of photograph 44629). This church was built in 1773 and considerably remodelled in 1881. Today it is the Rob Roy Information Centre, and the parish church is the one to the right of the photograph.

Excavations at Balquhidder's old church some years ago found a skeleton - its skull had been pierced by a musket ball. These were the remains of Stewart of Glenbuckie; on his way to join in the 1745 Jacobite uprising with MacGregor of Glencarnaig, he was either murdered or shot himself in the head at Leny Castle in Callander.

Balquhidder

The Old and New Churches. St Angus came to Balquhidder Glen in the 8th or 9th century; he built a stone oratory here, and stayed in the glen until he died. He was buried at the foot of Tom-nan-Aingeal, the Hill of Fire (the stone which covered his grave is now in the church, and there used to be a superstition that couples stood on the stone when they were married). About 1250, Labhran of Auchtubh, abbot of the Culdee monastery at Edinchip, built a small stone church over St Angus's grave, and in 1631 Lord Scone built another church, partially incorporating the ancient church – we can just see its belfry to the right of 44423. The present church was funded by David Carnegie of Stronvar in the 19th century.

Rob Roy (Robert MacGregor, 1671-1734) lies in the churchyard (B12301) here in the glen where as a young man he used to graze his sheep in the days before his fame. He raised a private army to protect himself against lawless gangs, and when he and his followers joined the Jacobite cause in the 1690s, they became outlaws. Legends soon grew of Rob Roy's daring, his hairsbreadth escapes, and his Robin Hood-like robbing the rich to give to the poor. Although arrested and sentenced to transportation in 1727, he was pardoned.

Tom-nan-Aingeal, the Hill of Fire, got its name because from ancient times up until as recently as the 19th century, twice a year on 1 May and 1 November (Beltane and Samhain) a fire was lit on the hill. All other fires in the village were put out, and the villagers climbed the hill to collect fresh fire to rekindle their hearths.

Above: BALQUHIDDER, THE OLD AND NEW CHURCHES
1899 44423

Right: BALQUHIDDER, ROB ROY'S GRAVE C1880 B12301

THE SOUTH WEST
Bishop's Hull, The Church 18
Bournemouth, St Peter's Church 26
Bristol, The Church of St Mary Redcliffe 20
Crantock, The Church 9, 10
Dartmouth, St Saviour's Church 13
Frampton, St Mary's Church 22
Glastonbury, St Michael's Tower 19
Kinson, St Andrew's Church 27
Lostwithiel, St Bartholomew's Church 12
Mortehoe, The Church 16
Morwenstow, The Church 8
Polzeath, St Enodoc's Church 11
Stinsford, St Michael's Church 23
Swimbridge, St James's Church 14, 15
Taunton, St Mary Magdalene's Church 17
Toller Porcorum, The Church of St Andrew and St Peter 21
Widecombe-in-the-Moor, The Church of St Pancras 13
Worth Matravers, St Nicholas's Church 24-25

LONDON AND THE SOUTH
Bentley, The Church 31
Bisham, All Saints' Church 53
Bonchurch, The Church of St Boniface 35-36
Bosham, Holy Trinity Church 43
Chertsey, St Peter's Church 40
Chingford, All Saints' Church 50
Eversley, St Mary's Church 32
Farnham, St Andrew's Church 38, 39
Goudhurst, St Mary's Church 48
Hanslope, St James's Church 57
Harrow-on-the-Hill, St Mary's Church 51
Hedsor, St Nicholas's Church 57
Hythe, St Leonard's Church 47
Kings Worthy, St Mary's Church 28-29, 30
Lullington, The Church 45
Medmenham, The Church of St Peter and St Paul 55
Newdigate, St Peter's Church 38
Reading, Christ Church 54
St Peter's, A Gravestone 49
Sandhurst, St Michael's Church 52
Shere, The Church 36
South Harting, The Church of St Mary and St Gabriel 41
Stoke Poges, St Giles's Church 56
Tillington, All Hallows' Church 42
Warnham, St Margaret's Church, A Gravestone 45
Winchester Cathedral
Winchfield, The Church of St Mary the Virgin 33
Worth, St Nicholas's Church 46
Wotton, The Church of St John the Evangelist 37
Wrotham, St George's Church 49
Yapton, The Church 44

WESTERN COUNTIES AND THE MIDLANDS
Abbey Dore, Holy Trinity and St Mary's Abbey Church 69

Ampthill, St Andrew's Church 89
Bedford, John Bunyan Statue 90
Bemerton, St Andrew's Church 59, 60
Bengeo, St Leonard's Church 93
Bibury, The Church 63
Blunham, The Church of St Edmund and St James 91
Bottesford, St Mary's Church 86
Bradford-on-Avon, St Laurence's Saxon Church 62
Bromham, St Nicholas's Church 61
Burton Lazars, St James's Church 85
Chedworth, St Andrew's Church 64
Deerhurst, The Saxon Church and Chapel 66
Earls Barton, All Saints' Church 82
Edwinstowe, The Church 88
Elstow, The Church 90
Hitchin, St Mary's Church 92
Horley, St Etheldreda's Church 68
Leicester, The Church of St Nicholas 84
Much Hadham, St Andrew's Church 94
Newark-on-Trent, St Mary's Church 87
Newport, The Church 75
Northampton, The Church of the Holy Sepulchre 81
Ollerton, Robin Hood Statue 88
Painswick, St Mary's Church 65
Pembridge, St Mary's Church 72
Quatford, The Church of St Mary Magdalene 73
Ross-on-Wye, St Mary's Church 70, 71
Rothwell, The Church, The Charnel House 83
Salisbury, The Church of St Thomas of Canterbury 58
Shorthampton, All Saints' Church 67
Shrewsbury, St Chad's Church 74
Sutton-on-Trent, All Saints' Church 88
Tettenhall, St Michael's Church 80
Tong, St Bartholomew's Church 76
Warwick, St Mary's Church 77
Willenhall, St Giles's Parish Church 78
Wolverhampton, St Peter's Church 79

EAST ANGLIA
Aldeburgh, The Church and Lifeboat 98
Blythburgh, The Church of the Holy Trinity 99
Booton, St Michael and All Angels' Church 104
Boston, St Botolph's Church 109, 110-111
Bramfield, St Andrew's Church 100
Castor, The Church of St Kyneburgha 108
Cawston, St Agnes's Church 103
Colchester, St Peter's Church 96
East Dereham, St Nicholas's Church 105
East Horndon, All Saints' Church 95
Grantchester, The Church of St Andrew and St Mary 106
Grantham, St Wulfram's Church 112
Little Maplestead, The Church of St John the Baptist 97
Pentlow, The Church of St George and St Gregory 95
Ranworth, St Helen's Church 102
Rickinghall Inferior, St Mary's Church 100

St Ives, Parish Church of All Saints 107
Stamford, St Mary's Church 109
Woolpit, St Mary's Church 101

THE NORTH
Adel, The Church of St John the Baptist 121
Ashbourne, The Church 118
Bakewell, All Saints' Church 119
Cartmel, The Priory Church 128
Chesterfield, The Church of St Mary and All Saints 120
Daresbury, All Saints' Church 114
Darley Dale, The Church 118
Escomb, The Saxon Church 135
Farndon, St Chad's Church 115
Gisburn, The Church 126
Grasmere, The Church of St Oswald 131
Heysham, St Peter's Church 125
Ilkley, The Church 122
Jarrow, St Paul's Church 136-137
Kendal, Holy Trinity Parish Church 129, 130
Kirk Braddan, The Old Church 127
Marton, The Parish Church of St James and St Paul 117
Masham, St Mary's Church 124
Nether Alderley, The Church 116
Penrith, St Andrew's Church 132, 133
Ribchester, Stydd Church 125
Selby Abbey, Gravedigger's Epitaph 122
Upleatham, The Church 134
Wallasey, The Church 113
York, Holy Trinity Church, Goodramgate 123

WALES
Abergavenny, St Mary's Church 138
Bodfari, The Church 146
Clynnogfawr, St Beuno's Church 143
Conwy, St Mary's Church 144
Gwbert-on-Sea, Mwnt Church 142
Llandough, St Dochdwy's Church 139
Llangennith, St Cenydd's Church 140
Pembrey, St Illtyd's Church 141
Rhosili, St Mary's Church 140
St Govan's Head, The Chapel 142

SCOTLAND
Alloway, The Kirk 148
Balquhidder, The Old and New Churches 154
Callander, The Church 153
Ecclefechan, Hoddam Church 147
Gourock, Old Gourock and Ashton Parish Church 149
Irvine, Parish Church 149
Linlithgow, St Michael's Church 150
Loch Achray, The Trossachs Church 2, 152
Muthill, The Old Church 151

The Francis Frith Collection Titles

www.francisfrith.com

The Francis Frith Collection publishes over 100 new titles each year. A selection of those currently available is listed below. For our latest catalogue please contact The Francis Frith Collection.
Town Books 96 pages, approximately 75 photos. **County and Themed Books** 128 pages, approximately 135 photos (unless specified). Pocket Albums are miniature editions of Frith local history books 128 pages, approximately 95 photos.

Accrington Old and New
Alderley Edge and Wilmslow
Amersham, Chesham and Rickmansworth
Andover
Around Abergavenny
Around Alton
Aylesbury
Barnstaple
Bedford
Bedfordshire
Berkshire Living Memories
Berkshire Pocket Album
Blackpool Pocket Album
Bognor Regis
Bournemouth
Bradford
Bridgend
Bridport
Brighton and Hove
Bristol
Buckinghamshire
Calne Living Memories
Camberley Pocket Album
Canterbury Cathedral
Cardiff Old and New
Chatham and the Medway Towns
Chelmsford
Chepstow Then and Now
Cheshire
Cheshire Living Memories
Chester
Chesterfield
Chigwell
Christchurch

Churches of East Cornwall
Clevedon
Clitheroe
Corby Living Memories
Cornish Coast
Cornwall Living Memories
Cotswold Living Memories
Cotswold Pocket Album
Coulsdon, Chipstead and Woodmanstern
County Durham
Cromer, Sheringham and Holt
Dartmoor Pocket Album
Derby
Derbyshire
Derbyshire Living Memories
Devon
Devon Churches
Dorchester
Dorset Coast Pocket Album
Dorset Living Memories
Dorset Villages
Down the Dart
Down the Severn
Down the Thames
Dunmow, Thaxted and Finchingfield
Durham
East Anglia Pocket Album
East Devon
East Grinstead
Edinburgh
Ely and The Fens
Essex Pocket Album
Essex Second Selection
Essex: The London Boroughs

Exeter
Exmoor
Falmouth
Farnborough, Fleet and Aldershot
Folkestone
Frome
Furness and Cartmel Peninsulas
Glamorgan
Glasgow
Glastonbury
Gloucester
Gloucestershire
Greater Manchester
Guildford
Hailsham
Hampshire
Harrogate
Hastings and Bexhill
Haywards Heath Living Memories
Heads of the Valleys
Heart of Lancashire Pocket Album
Helston
Herefordshire
Horsham
Humberside Pocket Album
Huntingdon, St Neots and St Ives
Hythe, Romney Marsh and Ashford
Ilfracombe
Ipswich Pocket Album
Isle of Wight
Isle of Wight Living Memories
King's Lynn
Kingston upon Thames
Lake District Pocket Album

Available from your local bookshop or from the publisher

The Francis Frith Collection Titles (continued)

Lancashire Living Memories
Lancashire Villages
Lancaster, Morecambe and Heysham Pocket Album
Leeds Pocket Album
Leicester
Leicestershire
Lincolnshire Living Memoires
Lincolnshire Pocket Album
Liverpool and Merseyside
London Pocket Album
Ludlow
Maidenhead
Maidstone
Malmesbury
Manchester Pocket Album
Marlborough
Matlock
Merseyside Living Memories
Nantwich and Crewe
New Forest
Newbury Living Memories
Newquay to St Ives
North Devon Living Memories
North London
North Wales
North Yorkshire
Northamptonshire
Northumberland
Northwich
Nottingham
Nottinghamshire Pocket Album
Oakham
Odiham Then and Now
Oxford Pocket Album
Oxfordshire
Padstow
Pembrokeshire
Penzance
Petersfield Then and Now

Plymouth
Poole and Sandbanks
Preston Pocket Album
Ramsgate Old and New
Reading Pocket Album
Redditch Living Memories
Redhill to Reigate
Richmond
Ringwood
Rochdale
Romford Pocket Album
Salisbury Pocket Album
Scotland
Scottish Castles
Sevenoaks and Tonbridge
Sheffield and South Yorkshire Pocket Album
Shropshire
Somerset
South Devon Coast
South Devon Living Memories
South East London
Southampton Pocket Album
Southend Pocket Album
Southport
Southwold to Aldeburgh
Stourbridge Living Memories
Stratford upon Avon
Stroud
Suffolk
Suffolk Pocket Album
Surrey Living Memories
Sussex
Sutton
Swanage and Purbeck
Swansea Pocket Album
Swindon Living Memories
Taunton
Teignmouth
Tenby and Saundersfoot
Tiverton

Torbay
Truro
Uppingham
Villages of Kent
Villages of Surrey
Villages of Sussex Pocket Album
Wakefield and the Five Towns Living Memories
Warrington
Warwick
Warwickshire Pocket Album
Wellingborough Living Memories
Wells
Welsh Castles
West Midlands Pocket Album
West Wiltshire Towns
West Yorkshire
Weston-super-Mare
Weymouth
Widnes and Runcorn
Wiltshire Churches
Wiltshire Living Memories
Wiltshire Pocket Album
Wimborne
Winchester Pocket Album
Windermere
Windsor
Wirral
Wokingham and Bracknell
Woodbridge
Worcester
Worcestershire
Worcestershire Living Memories
Wyre Forest
York Pocket Album
Yorkshire
Yorkshire Coastal Memories
Yorkshire Dales
Yorkshire Revisited

See Frith books on the internet at www.francisfrith.com

FRITH PRODUCTS & SERVICES

Francis Frith would doubtless be pleased to know that the pioneering publishing venture he started in 1860 still continues today. Over 140 years later, The Francis Frith Collection continues in the same innovative tradition and is now one of the foremost publishers of vintage photographs in the world. Some of the current activities include:

INTERIOR DECORATION

Today Frith's photographs can be seen framed and as giant wall murals in thousands of pubs, restaurants, hotels, banks, retail stores and other public buildings throughout the country. In every case they enhance the unique local atmosphere of the places they depict and provide reminders of gentler days in an increasingly busy and frenetic world.

PRODUCT PROMOTIONS

Frith products are used by many major companies to promote the sales of their own products or to reinforce their own history and heritage. Frith promotions have been used by Hovis bread, Courage beers, Scott's Porage Oats, Colman's mustard, Cadbury's foods, Mellow Birds coffee, Dunhill pipe tobacco, Guinness, and Bulmer's Cider.

GENEALOGY AND FAMILY HISTORY

As the interest in family history and roots grows world-wide, more and more people are turning to Frith's photographs of Great Britain for images of the towns, villages and streets where their ancestors lived; and, of course, photographs of the churches and chapels where their ancestors were christened, married and buried are an essential part of every genealogy tree and family album.

FRITH PRODUCTS

All Frith photographs are available framed or just as mounted prints and posters (size 23 x 16 inches). These may be ordered from the address below. From time to time other products - address books, calendars, table mats, etc - are available.

THE INTERNET

Already 100,000 Frith photographs can be viewed and purchased on the internet through the Frith website and a myriad of partner sites.

For more detailed information on Frith companies and products, look at this site:

www.francisfrith.com

See the complete list of Frith Books at: www.francisfrith.com
This web site is regularly updated with the latest list of publications from The Francis Frith Collection. If you wish to buy books relating to another part of the country that your local bookshop does not stock, you may purchase on-line.

For further information, trade, or author enquiries please contact us at the address below:
The Francis Frith Collection, Frith's Barn, Teffont, Salisbury, Wiltshire, England SP3 5QP.
Tel: +44 (0)1722 716 376 Fax: +44 (0)1722 716 881 Email: sales@francisfrith.co.uk

See Frith products on the internet at www.francisfrith.com

FREE PRINT OF YOUR CHOICE

Mounted Print
Overall size 14 x 11 inches (355 x 280mm)

CHOOSE A PHOTOGRAPH FROM THIS BOOK

Choose any Frith photograph in this book.

Simply complete the voucher opposite and return it with your remittance for £3.50
(to cover postage and handling) and we will print the photograph of your choice in SEPIA
(size 11 x 8 inches) and supply it in a cream mount with a burgundy rule line
(overall size 14 x 11 inches).

Offer valid for delivery to UK addresses only.

PLUS: **Order additional Mounted Prints at HALF PRICE - £8.50 each** (normally £17.00)
If you would like to order more Frith prints from this book, possibly as gifts for friends and
family, you can buy them at half price (with no additional postage and handling costs).

PLUS: **Have your Mounted Prints framed**
For an extra £14.95 per print you can have your mounted print(s) framed in an elegant
polished wood and gilt moulding, overall size 16 x 13 inches
(no additional postage and handling required).

IMPORTANT!

These special prices are only available if you use this form to order.

You must use the ORIGINAL VOUCHER on this page (no copies permitted).

We can only despatch to one UK address.

This offer cannot be combined with any other offer.

Send completed voucher form to:
The Francis Frith Collection, Frith's Barn, Teffont, Salisbury, Wiltshire SP3 5QP

Voucher for **FREE** and Reduced Price Frith Prints

*Please do not photocopy this voucher. Only the original is valid,
so please fill it in, cut it out and return it to us with your order.*

Picture ref no	Page no	Qty	Mounted @ £8.50	Framed + £17.00	Total Cost £
		1	Free of charge*	£	£
			£8.50	£	£
			£8.50	£	£
			£8.50	£	£
			£8.50	£	£
			£8.50	£	£

*Please allow 28 days for delivery.
Offer available to one UK address only*

* Post & handling	£3.50
Total Order Cost	**£**

Title of this book. . . . .

I enclose a cheque/postal order for £ . . . .
made payable to 'The Francis Frith Collection'

OR please debit my Mastercard / Visa / Maestro card,
details below

Card Number

Issue No (Maestro only)   Valid from (Maestro)

Expires   Signature

Name Mr/Mrs/Ms . . . .

Address . . . .

. . . .

. . . .

. . . . Postcode . . . .

Daytime Tel No . . . .

Email . . . .

ISBN 0-7537-1442-6   Valid to 31/12/09

Can you help us with information about any of the Frith photographs in this book?

We are gradually compiling an historical record for each of the photographs in the Frith archive. It is always fascinating to find out the names of the people shown in the pictures, as well as insights into the shops, buildings and other features depicted.

If you recognize anyone in the photographs in this book, or if you have information not already included in the author's caption, visit the Frith website at www.francisfrith.com and add your memories.

Our production team

Frith books are produced by a small dedicated team at offices in the converted Grade II listed 18th-century barn at Teffont near Salisbury, illustrated above. Most have worked with The Francis Frith Collection for many years. All have in common one quality: they have a passion for The Francis Frith Collection. The team is constantly expanding, but currently includes:

Paul Baron, Jason Buck, John Buck, Jenny Coles, Heather Crisp, David Davies, Natalie Davis, Louis du Mont, Isobel Hall, Chris Hardwick, Neil Harvey, Julian Hight, Peter Horne, James Kinnear, Karen Kinnear, Tina Leary, Stuart Login, Sue Molloy, Sarah Roberts, Kate Rotondetto, Eliza Sackett, Terence Sackett, Sandra Sampson, Adrian Sanders, Sandra Sanger, Julia Skinner, Lewis Taylor, Will Tunnicliffe, David Turner and Ricky Williams.